§ § §

PROMOTE MYSELF?
I'D RATHER EAT WORMS!

21 SIMPLE STEPS

To Confidently Tooting
Your Own Horn To Achieve
Your CAREER and LIFE GOALS

§ § §

Signe A. Dayhoff, Ph.D.

Promote Myself? I'd Rather Worms!
21 Simple Steps to Confidently Tooting Your Own
Horn to Achieve Your Career and Life Goals (2nd Edition)
by Signe A. Dayhoff, Ph.D.

Published by Effectiveness-Plus Publications LLC
80 Paseo de San Antonio
Placitas, New Mexico 87043-8735

Cover by Fotosearch Stock Photography & around 86
fiverr.com
Interior illustrations by Signe A. Dayhoff

ISBN: 978-0-9970168-8-8 (Print Ed.)

WHY THIS BOOK WAS WRITTEN

As someone who had no idea how to present and promote herself in order to take advantage of opportunities, I spun my wheels for years. I know that far too many of you too have not been doing the things you need to do to get what you want because of lack of information, guidance, essential skills, and resources (as well as problems with understandable self-consciousness, anxiety, and low self-confidence about presenting and promoting yourself).

Too many of us still believe that self-promotion is a taboo. But as Bonnie Marcus states in the *Politics of Promotion,* "Self-promotion is a leadership and political skill that is critical to master in order to navigate the realities of the workplace and position you for success."

Based upon years of research, this step-by-step book provides you with a detailed, effective, proven method that will significantly help you present and promote yourself, take advantage of opportunities, and achieve your job, advancement, career, and social goals. John D. Rockefeller said, "I always tried to turn every disaster into an opportunity."

Through examples, anecdotes, exercises, tools, and informational guidance, this book shows you what works, what does not, and why. It provides you with the enlightened path you need to get what you want. You *finally* can use confident, presenting and promoting yourself skills to find advancement, a new job, career, relationship, or your life direction.

Table of Contents

ACKNOWLEDGMENTS

This is to express my appreciation to all with whom I have studied, those experts I have interviewed who shared their experiences and suggestions, and the hundreds of business people and business students who so graciously participated in my years of research. I thank all of you, wishing I had the space to thank you all individually.

What all those people have reinforced in me is the absolute, essential need to promote yourself to achieve success of any kind. The following quotations capture that:

"All our dreams can come true if we have the courage to pursue them." - Walt Disney

"The whole secret of a successful life is to find out what is one's destiny to do, and then do it." - Henry Ford

"What seems to us as bitter trials are often blessings in disguise."- Oscar Wilde

"There is no surer way along the road to success than to follow in the footsteps of those who have reached it."- Anonymous

1

OPPORTUNITIES ARE WHAT YOU CREATE

"Opportunity is missed by most people because it is dressed in overalls and looks like work." – Thomas Edison

The raw material for creating opportunities is all around you. You encounter it every day. But, a lot of you are not attending to it and taking advantage of these opportunities because you are self-conscious, shy, or socially anxious. If you are emotionally "reluctant" to do it, it is likely because your social fears have you focused inwardly. That is, you are caught up in thoughts and beliefs that others will be evaluating you negatively if you try. If so, you likely are too busy trying to figure out how to cope with it to think about anything else. As a result, you are not looking outside yourself. You are just trying to cope and survive. You have to get outside yourself.

But once you can get those dysfunctional thoughts and feelings under control and can focus outside yourself, you can recognize that there is tremendous potential for *opportunities* out there. Once you are more comfortable with the idea of pursuing opportunities, then you need to learn how to

- Become aware of them when they present themselves
- Know what they can mean for you
- Understand how to follow through, to work with them to make them work for you. That is, how to fashion the clay to meet your artistic and practical goal.

Sounds simple enough ... but how actually are you supposed to know an "opportunity" when you see it? What is an "opportunity"? Then once you become aware of it and recognize it for what it is, what are you supposed to do with it? Most of us have never been specifically taught to spot "opportunities" much less what to do next, and after that, and after that.

"One secret of success in life is for a man [or woman] to be ready for his [or her] opportunity when it comes." – Benjamin Disraeli

In order to become aware of "opportunities," it is first necessary for you to become aware of yourself—your needs, wants, thoughts, beliefs, attitudes, and feelings— AND aware of what's going on in your environment. By discovering these factors, you become aware of what your "opportunity potential" is in general, how it comes into existence, how to spot it, and then how to take advantage of it.

Let's begin by examining "opportunity potential." *Opportunities* are a combination of favorable circumstances that you can make up. Those favorable circumstances—any one factor or a combination of these factors—can open the opportunity door. It all depends upon how alert you are to see it AND then act on it. Action is required. All the awareness and instruction on how to work with it are useless if you don't ACT on it.

This course is all about self-promotion so you might ask, "What has self-promotion to do with creating opportunities?" First, to tap into the vast reservoir of opportunity potential to create opportunities geared to achieving your goals, you have to be where people can

- See you
- Know you
- Know what you want
- Know what you have to offer.

This means when you're around these people, you have to know how to talk with them and present yourself. As you present yourself, you share things about yourself that direct people's attention to what you're interested in and seeking. Yes, I know, "self-promotion" has gotten a bad rep because some people do it immodestly, in a slick or arrogant fashion. That can be very off-putting. But it does *not* have to be any of these negative or manipulative things. In fact, when you take a closer look at it, you'll discover that you promote yourself in everything you do, from talking with a possible date, sharing ideas on a civic project, to telling a friend about an upcoming movie.

Self-promotion is managing the impression you make on others using your specific words, body language, and supporting materials. But it is also more. It also requires knowing the goal you want to achieve and the impression you want to create (intelligent, enthusiastic, expert, experienced, optimistic, serious, truthful, et al.) in order to achieve it. Optimism is important. As Winston Churchill stated, "A pessimist sees difficulty in every opportunity. An optimist sees opportunity in every difficulty." Furthermore, self-promotion is transforming that impression into action to finally achieve your goal. Simple and basic as that.

So when can you use self-promotion? Whenever you think it's appropriate—which is any time you want to achieve *any* goal (the list is nearly endless, especially as it pertains to jobs and careers):

- You promote yourself via your work to your boss and company
- You promote yourself to your organization
- You promote yourself to potential employers
- You promote yourself to your clients or customers in the marketplace
- You promote yourself to people you meet
- You promote yourself to individuals who may be potential mates.

In reality, *everything* you say and do either promotes you ... or does not promote you. It's all about making sure others see you and the qualities, abilities, skills, talents, and benefits you represent. It's all about your actively presenting yourself in the best possible light. It's all about confidently making yourself stand out so you can capture the other's attention and, thereby, the awaiting opportunities that will help you achieve your goals.

While that may sound a little scary initially, we will work through the process step-by-step so you will feel more confident, competent, and comfortable with it.

Finding and capturing "opportunities" isn't some deep, dark secret or complex process. Believe it or not, it is really quite straightforward. You can find, capture, and take advantage of opportunity potential simply by preparing yourself to do so. Preparation is the start of your step-by-baby-step process to achieving success.

- You begin by focusing on your awareness of yourself and your environment.
- You work on developing an inner vision of yourself by determining what strengths you have that others will value.
- You work on the impression you want to make on others so that it will have the greatest influence.
- You determine how your strengths match the qualities that are essential for successfully achieving your career or life goals.

Finally, to create career or life opportunities you need to work systematically and logically on your vision of what you want to achieve and precisely how you want to achieve it as well as mastering necessary techniques. You bolster your confidence by accomplishing every baby step in the process. Then, you practice your techniques and skills in accordance with your vision until it all becomes second nature to you. This prepares your path for your success.

The beauty of creating opportunities for yourself is that *you* are the one who has the control over the final product. That is, you determine what you want. You determine how you want to get it. You determine the resources you will use. You determine your timing. And you determine how you actually do achieve it. You can predict and control what you are going for and get it.

Having this control is a wonderful feeling. It is especially so for those who have any degree of reticence, reluctance, self-consciousness, shyness, or social anxiety. As you know, reticence, reluctance, self-consciousness, shyness, social anxiety, or not knowing the rules of the game can leave you feeling buffeted about by the fates and out of control of your daily life and your destiny. This can leave you frustrated, angry, disappointed, and disillusioned.

While the process I am about to show you is simple and straightforward, you will need to fully immerse yourself in it in order for you to fully benefit from it. And what are the many ways you can benefit? You can create jobs, job advancement, relationships, Internet business, or any marketplace opportunities for yourself and then act on them. You can profitably chart your life and get where you want to go in the most direct, confident, and simplest way possible.

But never forget that "Opportunity does not knock. It presents itself than you have to beat down the door." – Kyle Chandler

ORIENTATION

You know the ancient saying: "Give me a fish, and I will eat today. Teach me to fish, and I will eat for the rest of my life." This book teaches you not only how to "fish" but also how to survive and dynamically succeed in your job, career, relationships, and life.

However, your survival-to-success results from more than just what you do. It results from the complex interaction of your thoughts, feelings, and behavior with your environment. Because of this, sections of this book are devoted to mental preparedness. The degree of your preparedness translates into the degree of your success. Your success begins in your mind.

As you have found in working on your reticence, reluctance, shyness, self-consciousness, social anxiety etc., competence alone cannot achieve your desired goal of creating career and life opportunities. You also need appropriate mental conditioning, motivation, and savvy.

Consequently, you maximize your results and your benefits by doing the many exercises the book presents, answering the thought questions, taking notes, and practicing the techniques. Your key to success - to achieving your goals - is the 3 Ps: **P**ersistence, **P**atience, and **P**ractice!

Your ACTIVE participation and involvement are not only required but also essential.

SUCCESS

"Success" is a word that is thrown around a lot. How do you know if you've really achieved "success"? You are successful when you have (1) learned what to look for to achieve your goals and when you (2) actively seek out the means to do it. Specifically, you have learned how to recognize potential opportunities, then create and wisely use your opportunities to your advantage.

Success requires learning that you cannot wait

passively for opportunities to drop into your lap. You cannot sit back waiting for opportunity to knock on your door. You must diligently go out into the world to see what's going on. You must diligently follow the steps necessary to getting what you want in the process. You must actively choose to adapt to prevailing circumstances and expand your horizons in order to survive and thrive. Your success is accomplishing your goals confidently, efficiently, and effectively.

Remember: "Success" is your intention converted into action-toward-achievement.

KEYSTONE

I believe that the opportunities to achieve your goals and satisfy your wants are unlimited. Doors are constantly opening for those waiting prepared and ready to go through them. Fascinating challenges present themselves everywhere all the time for those with awareness and eyes to see them.

As Tom Peters, business management author, says, "If the window of opportunity appears, don't pull down the shade." New frontiers bound, just around the corner. You can start seizing and tailoring those opportunity factors to your plan *now!*

2

YOU MAY BE AN ENDANGERED SPECIES

Those who successfully achieve their goals design and execute their career and life development. They create their opportunities for themselves. They know that without continuing efforts toward career and life development they can and likely will become an "endangered species" in all the aspects of their world that matter to them.

Are you really getting what you want from your job, career, marketplace, social or personal relationships? Or are you just somewhat content with the *status quo*? Are you coasting along, frustrated with where you are? Are you doing only what is sufficient to maintain yourself even though you want something else? If so, you may be in danger of becoming extinct—losing out on what's important to you.

What sorts of things can make you "endangered"?

- You feel only relatively competent because too often your job requires interpersonal skills you feel you do not have so you hide.

- You are a conscientious worker but avoid some

social situations, small talk, making presentations, networking, public speaking, asserting yourself, expressing disagreement or criticism, talking to authority figures, thus diminishing your chances of being seen.

- You are not always comfortable that you know what is expected of you so you don't speak up, asking questions or expressing opinions or facts.
- You have built up a generally positive past-performance record but may have changed jobs frequently to avoid various interpersonal tasks so you don't feel you can promote yourself as expert or even someone experienced.
- Your rapport with your colleagues may be less than desirable because of decreased social interaction, which leaves you an unknown entity.
- Your boss may respect your efforts but does not see you as a go-getter because you do not share your work-related achievements.
- You feel it is immodest, crass, arrogant, or inappropriate to make your achievements known. You believe people should be able to detect them on their own.
- People you'd like to get to know socially, perhaps personally, don't know because you don't seek them out, approach them, or indicate your interest in getting to know them.
- You are reluctant to toot your own horn in any way to promote yourself.

As a result, while you may be giving your all and doing what you think is expected in a practical sense, chances are great that you are not seen as a visible and credible work or social contributor. Not being visible and credible to those who matter, to those who have influence and make decisions, puts you at risk. That is, you are at risk not necessarily because of what you have done—and done right, but because of what you have *not* done—or done right.

MEETING THE DEMANDS OF SURVIVAL

As conducting daily business becomes more complex and competitive, your survival in your world, but especially the work world, requires not only your attention, but also your *selective* attention. This is the same type of attention you have paid to your experience of reticence, reluctance, isolation, anonymity, self-consciousness, shyness, or social anxiety.

However, with respect to self-consciousness and the others, too often you focused your attention selectively on the *negative*. That is because your thoughts and feelings were negative and you likewise directed your attention in that direction. This, thus, reinforced your feelings of discomfort, inadequacy, and fear about promoting yourself. Like recovering from self-consciousness and other social fears, achieving your career and life goals requires you substitute the positive for the negative.

Your creating opportunities through self-promotion—making yourself known—requires that you learn to re-focus on what you *can* do—on what is possible. No longer can you feel or say that you can't accomplish what you want, that Fate is against you, or that opportunities never come your way.

ACHIEVING CAREER GOALS

What makes this especially important is that every year millions of people are trying to improve their career situation. However, on average in a good year only 25% will be successful in finding those desired new jobs, job advancement, or have a profitable business on-or offline Of course, this figure differs significantly depending upon the state of the economy. However, by knowing what to do to promote yourself, taking advantage of potential opportunities, and acting on that knowledge, you *significantly* increase the odds in your favor.

If you want to achieve career goals, you have to know what your "career" really is. In general, your career is made up of several things. It is a combination of flexible skills and a series of related work experiences. Career development looks at what you do and have done. It involves focusing on your work-related wants and improving your methods of satisfying them.

Career development requires your changing your behavior to meet your goals—adapting to new circumstances. Goal achievement is a learned skill that is based on observable, measurable, and analyzable behavior laid out in a series of steps. It is *not* based on some set of ideal personality characteristics or traits that only a select few possess. Instead, it involves a change process wherein you hone and perfect your self-promotion skills and patterns of goal-achievement behavior.

Career development is highly individualized. This means it is whatever you make it to be. *You're* the one who directs *your* efforts toward *your* creating *your* own choice of opportunities which enhance *your* career development.

Another way to think about these opportunities is that they are your *expectations about future prospects*. When you promote yourself to create the opportunities you want, you create career success possibilities and probabilities. In other words, your expectations forge your making yourself known, which fosters your development, which then achieves your goals and creates your success.

Whether you are a steno pool secretary, computer assembly line worker, retail clerk, independent consultant, sales representative, engineer, teacher, lawyer, physician, small business owner, manager, or recent college- or trade school graduate, you need to promote yourself to develop yourself in your career. For example, gradually young workers are recognizing that the economy will always require trained, experienced people for the construction trade.

With this in mind the PBS program "This Old House," began nurturing young people starting out in the building trades in part because of the dearth of these professionals today. Those who were aware of opportunities and had specific career goals in mind quickly made themselves available as volunteers for the show. Their interest, enthusiasm, can-do attitudes, and work created for them influential relationships and made them visible. They can later positively expand on those relationships and that visibility.

About 90% of your career development is the result of how you perceive and work with your day-to-day job experience toward your goals. Specifically, it's how you see and respond to specific events, contacts, relationships, and general working climate. It's how you make yourself recognizable (that's *visible* and *credible*) for what you do. It is always keeping in mind that everything you do is a stepping stone toward meeting your objectives and getting what you want.

Regarding meeting objectives, Former Prime Minister of India, Jawaharlal Nehru said, "Failure only comes when we forget our ideals, objectives, and principles."

On that same note, Vic Conant, President and CEO of Nightingale-Conant Corp, the premier publisher of audio personal development programs, echoes this: "Failing to meet your objectives, regardless of what they are, is a *choice*, because something else has been given a higher priority. If you fail, it is because you choose to fail."

Likewise, if you succeed, you chose to succeed. "Objectives" are the incremental steps that you need to achieve in order to meet your final goal.

Furthermore, "The reward for work well done is the opportunity to do more." – Jonas Salk

3

GETTING ON THE OPPORTUNITY BANDWAGON

Playwright George Bernard Shaw wrote, in his play *Mrs. Warren's Profession*, "The people who get on in this world are the people who get up and look for the circumstances they want, and, if they can't find them, make them."

THE SKY'S THE LIMIT

You need to ask yourself, "How opportunity-aware am I?" "How willing am I to do what's necessary to create opportunities?" In order to meet your goal-achievement expectations, you have to foster certain behaviors and attitudes. That is, you must

- Feel motivated to achieve your goals
- Feel competent to meet self-promotion and development challenges
- Be prepared to meet those challenges
- Know concretely and specifically what your goals are
- Be open to different ways to achieve your goals
- Have a systematic, step-by-step plan of objectives

to achieve each goal

- Consider making yourself known, liked, and trusted as your primary path to getting what you want.

PERCEPTIONS OF YOU

How successful you are in creating and developing your opportunities and your career depends, to a great degree, on perception. That is your perception of yourself as well as the perceptions of you by others. Ask yourself the following:

(Have an 8 ½" x 11" notebook available in which to answer these questions, and others throughout the course, as fully as possible.)

1. How do I see myself? What are your outstanding characteristics?
2. In what ways do I see myself as reasonably competent and capable or ineffective and inadequate?

Your success depends on how those around you, both inside and outside of the organization, perceive you. Ask yourself the following:

1. How do they see me? As a conscientious worker or one who cannot be counted on to do what is required? Explain what you mean.
2. How responsible and dependable am I? Give examples.
3. Do I know for a fact that decision makers are aware how hard I work and what positive results I have contributed to the company? How do I know?

The painful truth is that how the world *appears*-to-be very often becomes how "we think" the world *is*. That is, how you and others perceive you in your job literally creates your work reality. Since what you do affects others' perception of you, you want to behave in a manner befitting the perception you want them to have of you.

If you want to be perceived as success-oriented, you must do things that suggest growth and development. To perform your job by doing only what is necessary or only those tasks not demanding interpersonal interaction is to be perceived as "just a worker," just a cog in a wheel, indistinguishable from all the other cogs. This is a person stuck, at risk, and, therefore, endangered.

Your career survival-to-success requires that you hold certain beliefs and perform certain behaviors. Specifically, you need to believe and to demonstrate to those who pay you for your services that you are a unique resource, valuable to the organization.

It's imperative that you believe—and show—that you are not just another warm body in the organization. You need to believe and show that you are not interchangeable with other people in your job category. You are not just "another" computer analyst or a teacher clone.

Furthermore, you need to believe that you are more than the sum of your present job experience, daily performance, skills, and aptitudes added together.

How do you make these beliefs happen? One method used by athletes is to visualize yourself where you want to be, actually see yourself in that situation, doing what that person does, and doing it successfully. Where you want to be must be concrete and specific, something you can see, feel, and taste, so you can make the visualization real.

You do this by determining what steps you must go through to get from where you are to where you want to go. In your visualization you picture yourself achieving each objective step. To do this successfully you must first know concrete, specific things about yourself:

(*Answer these questions as fully as possible in your notebook but you will want to come back to this as you develop who and what you are and what you want.*)

1. Who are you as it relates to your job/career goal?
2. What skills, talents, aptitudes, and resources do you offer?
3. Where do you want to go now and in the future?
4. How are you going to get there? By what path? Using what resources?
5. What do you want and need in order to accomplish it?

Of course, all this is more than you can expect yourself to know as you begin the process. But what you absolutely must have at the start of the process is conviction. It is the conviction that *what you do, you do well, and that nobody else does it quite the same way you do it.* It is imperative that you know you have something to offer to the organization that is valuable and unique.

"Okay," you say, "I guess I believe that I am valuable and unique. Yeah, I believe I can bring to my job some combination of things that no one else can. But so what if I know it? The company has to know it too. So how do I convince them, the powers that be, that this is true?"

"All of us need to understand the importance of branding [promoting visibility, credibility, and name recognition]. We are CEOs of our own companies: Me Inc. To be in in business today, our most important job is to be head marketer for the brand called You." - Tom Peters.

NEED FOR VISIBILITY

The very first thing you must do in order to be seen as valuable and unique is, literally, **be seen**. This may sound pretty obvious, but it is not, really. At present, you may be
invisible. You may be regarded only as a face in the crowd, and not as a useful, contributing individual with potential for more.

If so, you are just part of a mass. You are like one of the dots making up a newspaper photograph. To be seen, to make yourself stand out from other job holders, you must do something to create visibility.

Visibility results from a combination of factors such as ability, performance, and recognition. Visibility is a significant factor in creating advancement opportunities because it makes you noticeable. But it is being "noticeable" in a special and positive way.

For example, although running nude through the executive dining room will give you exposure, it is unlikely to make your face memorable, in any profitable way, when promotion time rolls around.

JOCKEYING FOR ORGANIZATIONAL ATTENTION

It is important to remember that as a job-holder, you are only part of that large crowd of competent peers who are vying for organizational attention. Organizational attention is catching and holding the decision maker's eye. This attention is critical. It can result in raises, promotions, sponsorship, or hanging onto your job in times of change.

Do not think that merely being competent and/or a good performer guarantees your organizational career survival-to-success. It does not. Nothing gives a 100% guarantee. But some things make your goal achievement and career success that much more likely.

In the organization, as in life in general, survival belongs to the fittest. It goes to the individuals and species that can adapt best to the changing environment. Survival means accommodating yourself to meet new requirements.

Remember what it was like in school when you got a new teacher, or at work when you got a new boss? Suddenly, there were new expectations of you, new ways of doing old things, and new rules to follow. Everything felt up in the air and uncomfortable. You weren't sure what the new guidelines were with this person. Consequently, you had to make a decision. You could choose to do what you always had done or you could choose to behave according to the dictates of the new situation. The fact was that your survival as a student or job holder depended upon your adapting to the situation. As a result, in general, you found a way to adapt. Become adept at adapting to new situations is essential.

YOUR IMAGE AS A SUCCESS MODEL

Your goal in creating visibility is to make yourself appear as a success model. You want to appear as representative of the organization, but special. Thus, if the organization were to commission a poster to recruit winners, you would be the model for it.

Your qualifications for this *Success Model* would be described as

- One of us
- Most of us
- Best of us.

One of Us: It is important to appear as a team member, willing to work with others and cooperate to achieve team organizational goals. You must appear loyal to your team, your supervisor, and the organization. Furthermore, you must appear oriented to company goals, rather than oriented to your personal goals only. Of course, you're oriented toward your personal goals (making a paycheck, having a long satisfying career) but that must not be your "image." You must be seen as a "company person." That is, one whose goal at work is to do the best for the company.

The most powerful success image is to be empathetic to your team and the company and not self-centered in any way. Specifically, your image needs to be sensitive to and involved in the needs of others, with the company's profit making and survival your primary work goal.

Most of Us: It is important to be seen as upholding the organization's values, attitudes, and goals. These represent the majority perspective. Being congruous with organizational means and ends indicates that you operate the way others do in the organization. It does *not* necessarily mean, however, that you conform to a company personality stereotype. In most cases, neither strict conformity nor nonconformity creates positive visibility for you. However, "conformity" of a sort might be emphasized and praised at an organization like the FBI and IBM, and less so at an organization like Apple and Google.

Best of Us. It is important to appear as "competent-plus." That is, you need to be better than your peers in some demonstrable way. For example, you can appear competent-plus by

- Being aware of your environment and its needs
- Having and using specialized knowledge or skills
- Taking on undesirable but necessary assignments
- Providing quality and productivity
- Looking for more responsibility
- Developing yourself for advancement
- Sharing your resources unselfishly
- Bringing others along in the organization
- Being seen and valued as a skilled, responsible, and dependable go-getter.

Upward movement in organizations tends to be based on this competence-plus model. Specifically, advancement (also referred to as "vertical organizational mobility") is rarely based on good performance alone. Likewise, it is rarely based on sponsorship visibility alone. Instead, career advancement tends to be based on a mix of good performance, which is made visible, and assistance from some organizationally influential other person who helps make you visible. Either way, you must achieve positive visibility AND credibility to open opportunity doors for yourself and advance.

SUCCESS MYTHOLOGY PROBLEMS

Success is something for which you are expected to strive for most of your life. It's considered to be inherent in your goals. But what is "success"? For most of us it means "achieving something desired, planned, or attempted," such as gratification, fame, prosperity, superiority, or victory.

But, as you know, striving for and achieving success in any field of endeavor is not always easy. There are nearly always obstacles in your path. And contrary to popular opinion, these obstacles are not just factors outside yourself. Internal factors can significantly hinder your progress as well.

For example, your beliefs and attitude about success and how it operates in the world are too often based on popular myths. These myths are distortions or generalizations. Believing them can sabotage you. This belief too often results in shooting yourself in your foot. That's self-sabotage. It makes your achieving success nearly impossible. This is especially true with respect to what you do to market your business or promote yourself in any situation.

Here are a few Success Myths that you need to not only ignore but also counter:

- **"Success is universal"** - Success is really whatever you individually define it to be. It's dependent upon how you structure your goal, what resources you use to achieve it, and how you measure the results.

- **"Success is what others define it to be"** - Again, your success is *your* definition alone. It can range from feeling satisfied, attracting your ideal clients, developing social relationships you want, getting referrals, to having all the high-status accessories that some people feel symbolize "having made it" in life. And maybe it's in your creating a sense of happiness.

  As President Franklin D. Roosevelt stated, "Happiness lies in the joy of achievement and the thrill of creative effort."

- **"Only some people can be successful because they have the right background, connections, or education"** - While this often appears to be true, and none of these things likely hurt, success comes to those who want something badly enough to do whatever it takes (within their own value system) to get it. It comes to those who create a logical, step-by-step plan, access necessary resources, and actively follow their plan consistently with patience and persistence, creating visibility and credibility, and correcting course according to new circumstances.

- **"Success results from working an excess of 40 hours per week"** - Achieving what you want comes from doing what's necessary and doing it right. Working 60 hours a week doing the wrong things doesn't create success. Instead, it creates stress, fatigue, and frustration.

Management guru Peter Drucker says, "Being efficient is doing the job right, but being effective is doing the right job."

- **"Successful people manage to avoid mistakes"** - There's no such thing as perfection. Everyone makes mistakes ... LOTS of them. This is because most of your learning is by trial and error. There's a saying that an executive who makes only 50 percent of his/her decisions correctly is still an effective, successful leader.

The primary difference between successful and unsuccessful people is that successful people don't keep repeating their mistakes. You know what they say about people who make the same mistake over and over and expect a different result each time they do it. According to President Barak Obama, "The real test is not whether you avoid this failure, because you won't. It's whether you let it harden or shame you into inaction, or whether you learn from it; whether you choose to persevere."

It's a mistake to think that mistakes are bad. Another way to think about them is that the more you try different things toward achieving your goal (trials) and the sooner you try them, the more mistakes (errors) you'll make but the sooner you are likely to achieve your goal. It's mistakes that help you learn what works and what doesn't and keep on the right track.

As Thomas A. Edison said regarding creating the electric lightbulb, "I haven't failed. I've just found 10,000 ways that didn't work."

- **"Successful people are those who pull themselves up by their bootstraps all by themselves"** - In fact, no one becomes a success without some assistance along the way - whether it's personal guidance, financial or educational assistance. Getting assistance does not detract from your personal achievement. In fact, getting and using assistance effectively, whether in marketing or in any other area, is the mark of a smart and successful person.

- **"Success is merely a matter of luck"** - While chance may play a part in your achieving your goals, most of what you achieve is the result of knowledge, application, and hard work—Churchill's prescription of "blood, sweat, and tears."

  Remember that Edison also said, "Success is the result of 90 percent perspiration and 10 percent inspiration."

  Success doesn't just fall into your lap. You can't wait for opportunity to knock on your door. Success results from your being prepared for it, having a plan you actively follow, seeking opportunities, and working with them.

- **"There's only one way to achieve success"** - Granted, there are no specific rules for achieving any particular success, but there may be methods which are more useful to attaining your goals. Of course, each situation requires an approach appropriate to it and one with which you are personally comfortable. Precisely how you achieve anything is going to be different for each person and each circumstance, but there will be some basic commonalities.

- **"Being successful makes life trouble-free"** - Don't you wish that were so! Life is never "trouble-free" no matter what you achieve. There are always external and internal issues with which to deal. You will always have good and bad moments, ups and downs, situations which don't work out as you want, people who disappoint you. While success (goal achievement) gets you what you want in one area of your life for some period of time, it's not (alas) all-encompassing ... or forever. Your continuing feeling of success requires you keep applying your self-promotion techniques and procedures to each goal you wish to achieve.

It's essential that you recognize and enjoy each success (large or small objective or goal) as it comes for what it says about you and what it gives you. Furthermore, it's essential that you see how you're responsible for your achievements and feel good about yourself for what you've done. This creates true self-confidence and productive self-promotion beliefs and skills on which you can build for achieving your next goal.

What exactly is *self-confidence?* It is a control-related belief that you have the ability to *manage* particular kinds of activities, *mobilize* your motivation, *control* your cognitive and emotional reactions to it, and *achieve* your desired outcomes—better known as *SUCCESS!*

Put another way, self-confident is being the best you can be with who you are and what you have. This means you choose to mirror yourself, as opposed to someone else, because you *value* and are *comfortable with* yourself. In other words, the path you follow is designed by your inner core and not by what others do or expect of you, what appears to work for them, or what you think you "should" do. It is also the belief that no matter what you are faced with, you will be able to deal with it by doing what you need to do. You rise to the occasion. You meet the challenge. Specifically, you must be "willing" to do whatever is necessary whether you actually do it or not.

You absolutely need to de-mythologize "success" for yourself. Once you do, you can cast aside those internal roadblocks and create realistic, focused, achievable, measurable plans to accomplish what you desire in both your business and personal life. That not only builds on but also strengthens and reinforces your self-confidence.

TAKING THAT EXTRA STEP

Economic times tend to determine what organizations want in employees. For example, while organizations in the past valued and rewarded job holders who did exactly and only what their job descriptions dictated, organizations today tend to look for and reward company members who go that extra step. They look for and reward those who demonstrate a willingness to do and be more than what is required. In general, in good economic times the specialist is favored.

But in tight economic times the generalist tends to be favored over the specialist. But as the economy improves and grows, specialists are often more highly sought.

Irrespective of the economy, organizations look for and reward those who have *visible*

- Aspirations
- Work commitment
- A sense of organizational responsibility and loyalty.

In fact, among individuals who are seen as qualified for a position, the one most likely to be selected is the one who has developed the most extensive degree of visibility, credibility, contact help, and influence. As a result, the competent but invisible job holder is likely to become an endangered species.

Again: You do not have to become an endangered species. You can *control* the direction of your career development. You can *choose* to have your career succeed.

Remember: What you are, what you do, and what you become are the result of your career opportunity creation choices.

Since the key to your career survival-to-success is *visibility*, you need to consciously choose to become visible. You need to put your self-consciousness, shyness, reticence, reluctance, or social anxiety behind you. I know that may sound daunting, but it does not have to be. You can do that—and so much more—by simply following the plan I have designed for you, starting with Chapter 3.

Henry David Thoreau once wrote, "If you have built castles in the air, you need not be lost; that is where they should be. Now put the foundations under them."

4

FOCUSING ON GOAL ACHIEVEMENT

Questions you need to think about: *(Answer these questions as fully as possible in a notebook.)*

1. What are your career goals, generally and specifically?
2. What specific, actual steps are necessary to achieve them?
3. What resources will you need to achieve them?
4. How can you make yourself more visible?
5. How would you describe what you need to put in your plan to achieve visibility?
6. How willing are you to talk with strangers and make small talk?
7. How willing are you to create contacts to create visibility and credibility and pursue opportunities?

MAKING CONNECTIONS

There are many ways to achieve visibility, create credibility, and act on opportunities. One way to achieve visibility is to create contacts. Contacts are individuals who possess the information, resources, or influence you want in order to achieve your goals. Contacts can be any person with whom you are acquainted. You can get in touch with them. This means that potentially anyone can be useful to you.

It means also that in order to make contacts you need to

- Clarify and specify what you want from others
- Be open to meeting and talking with strangers
- Qualify contacts for what they have and what you want
- Be willing to respond to their issues or problems by offering help
- Be willing to ask for help
- Seek out specific people for specific goal achievement.

In a nutshell: You see it! You want it! You go after it!

Making contacts is what opportunity creators (successful people) do. In fact, one of the most important characteristics of self-made millionaires and other successful people is that they create opportunities for themselves by making contacts through networking everywhere, all the time. They do not wait around in hope that opportunity will grab them by the collar, screaming, "Here I am!" ... because they *know* it will not.

As Harvey Mackay, *New York Times* best-selling author of *Dig Your Well Before You're Thirsty*, repeatedly demonstrates, networking is the primary and best way to gain access to friends, jobs, health, legal, and financial information, hobbies, services, and career development. Whatever circumstances you seek, whatever opportunities you desire, you can achieve them through networking to make contacts.

According to writer Susan Rittscher in *Forbes*, "Successful entrepreneurs know that the lifeblood of their business is found in making the right connections. Whether it is for potential business alliances, sales, marketing, supply chain management or just to escape the loneliness of being a solopreneur, making connections is vital for business growth."

Networking entrepreneur Jerry Rubin, when he started Studio 54, a nightclub where A-listers flocked, echoed this in his business philosophy: "You can meet anyone you want to know through one or two people. And do not be surprised if you meet someone who changes your life."

While everyone has heard of networking, many people avoid engaging in it because they mistakenly believe it to be using people or trying to sell them something. On the contrary, "true networking" is all about sharing and helping. It is the active process of exchanging information and assistance with others in order to build and maintain relationships.

Note: The essence of networking is **being seen**, **known**, **trusted**, and **liked** in order to create mutually beneficial relationships.

In Napoleon Hill's 1937 classic, *Think and Grown Rich,* Hill described a peer-to-peer mentoring group which helps members solve problem through the input and advice of other members. W. Clement Stone, founder of *Success!* Magazine, crystallized networking in the concept of the MasterMind Group: "To achieve your mission in life, you must seek out and work with other talented, dedicated, experienced people … in harmony." The result of networking is a collective or team of supportive members to whom you can provide informational, instrumental, emotional, and supportive assistance and from whom you can receive the same when needed.

Networking is built on the principle of reciprocity, a powerful norm in Western cultures. Participants in a relationship expect to give as well as receive. If there is no mutual benefit forthcoming, the interaction will feel unsatisfying and incomplete and will likely cease.

A classic example is when auto magnate Lee Iacocca was out of a job, fired from Ford Motor Company in the 1980s, what did he do? Did he dust off his résumé and head on down to his local unemployment office or executive placement agency? No! He talked to his associates and cronies. Over lunch—over the phone. He talked with close personal friends, including George Bennett of State Street Investment Corporation and Claud Kirk, ex-governor of Florida.

Together, Bennett and Kirk talked with Richard Dilworth, a board member of Chrysler Corporation at the time They suggested to Dilworth that since the financially embarrassed Chrysler had a leadership problem and they had a leadership solution in Iacocca, they all should get together over lunch to discuss it.

And they did. Over a quiet luncheon of raw oysters at the Hotel Pontchartrain, Chrysler offered Iacocca its presidency. He accepted it, at his former annual salary.

If the process sounds straight-forward and simple,

that is because it is. Iacocca

1. Knew what he wanted to achieve
2. Approached his contacts
3. His contacts, in turn, acted as sponsors for him
4. They passed on his qualifications to Chrysler decision makers.
5. They acted as cheerleaders, creating visibility for Iacocca.

In no time at all, the former head of Ford was in a new position of his choosing, one befitting his status and bank account.

This process also works in reverse. What worked for Iacocca would work similarly for his associates, friends, and cronies. Iacocca would act as a contact for them. It is important to remember that in this relationship while the other person is a contact for you, you are a contact for the other person as well.

Whether you are aware of it or not, everyone has a basic network of contacts that has evolved over time. It is made up of *primary* contacts, such as family and friends, who have similar attitudes, values, beliefs, interests, and contacts It is also made up of *secondary* contacts, such as acquaintances, work colleagues, clients, and service people, who have diverse attitudes, values, beliefs, interests, and contacts.

Each contact is a potential resource because of:

- Who they are
- What they do
- What they know
- Whom they know
- Who knows them (especially important because

this refers to their own network which you can tap into through your contact).

Each of your primary and secondary network groups represents two levels of contact: Those you can contact directly and immediately and those you can contact indirectly and over time because they are through someone else. It has been suggested that if you know fifty people on a first-name basis and so do all the people you know, you immediately have available 2,500 friends of friends. The more friends and associates you have, the greater is the number of people exponentially to whom you have access.

Today in the era of e-mail, Google, Smart Phones, and social media you can reach networking contacts with only a click or two—even more quickly than psychologist Stanley Milgram demonstrated with his "small world"—six degrees of separation—experiments in the 1960s using people carrying letters. In the 1960s Milgram found that it took only five or six contacts (but lots of time) to reach the specific person of interest. Today it can be minutes, hours, or perhaps only a day or two.

It is important to keep in mind that networking does **not** mean going to any and every business or social gathering because it has "networking." Instead, you need to choose your gatherings carefully so that they represent likely avenues to reach your goals. For example, you would choose gatherings to be attended by people with information, abilities, experience, or expertise you want to tap into, and/or people of influence.

Furthermore, whenever possible, you would want to

- Have a solid sense of who will be there that you may wish to contact
- Know something about them (what they do, what they likely know, and their interests)
- Why specifically you want to create a relationship with them.

You are likely to be more successful in your networking for creating visibility and opportunities for yourself if you build your networking contacts with *two* goals in mind.

1. First is to make yourself well-known by providing assistance to others in need, and doing so *without* expectation of reward.
2. Second is to have a specific goal in mind for which you are seeking assistance.

Erroneously, and unfortunately, many people tend to equate *only* the second goal with networking and then act on that alone. That is doomed to failure. Seeking only to get help for yourself from others is ineffective, inefficient, and unproductive. Moreover, it does not create a positive impression. When you don't create a mutually beneficial relationship with your contact, the negative word can spread, making you seem selfish and unhelpful.

Note: It is essential that you *never* use your networking to try to sell yourself, your service or product or make the other person a client.

Volunteering your help to others is by far the more important of the two networking goals because it fosters good will, expands your sphere of influence, and creates a positive impression of you. You are seen as a generous, reliable, and valued resource for your skills, talents, abilities, values, tips, advice, information, referrals, and leads. You become both visible and credible. That's a success- and opportunity-bolstering combination.

Remember: Networking is all about creating positive visibility first.

Fostering good will is an essential part of your networking strategies. But while just helping is necessary, it is not sufficient. Specifically, when you help others (whether it is an individual or an organization, like the Chamber of Commerce or the Rotary), you need to go one step beyond. That is, you need to *do more* than just what is required or expected. In other words, you need to over-deliver.

Furthermore, you need to do so *without* any obvious ulterior, "what's-in-it-for-me" motive. This means you are helping because you want to share, **not** because you openly desire a *quid pro quo* for it. This whole-hearted altruism engenders a sense of trust and gratitude in those with whom you network. This makes networking a solid basis for your getting visibility and referrals.

According to Rick Frishman and Jill Lublin in their book *Networking Magic*, you should start your *good-will-building* networking before you need to look for information. In addition, it is essential that you keep your two networking goals separate so it does not appear you are trying to manipulate anyone to get something.

But, remember, for you to be this valued resource to

your network you have to know what strengths and resources you have to offer. This means you have to be aware of your skills, attributes, abilities, information, as well as your connections. Too often people are not aware of the diversity, depth, and extent of what they have to offer. Unless you make a careful evaluation of yourself, you may be selling yourself short as a resource and making yourself less attractive as a contact.

Too much humility and modesty can act as obstacles in this assessment. You must see yourself as having strengths that others want and value. You must believe in your heart of hearts that you are a unique blend of background, values, work and life experiences from which others can and will benefit. *You should commit the follow to memory until it becomes second nature.*

Networking requires that you:

- Take the initiative to introduce yourself and talk to others
- Be open, approachable, positive, and enthusiastic
- Meet strangers and make small talk (if necessary, learn how to do this)
- Look for ways to create similarities because similarities form bonds
- Help and share whenever and wherever
- Accept responsibility for your actions
- Make no negative assumptions, don't jump to conclusions
- Don't prejudge people as not helpful because you never know
- Value yourself and what you have to offer to others

- Keep expanding your network to increase number and diversity
- Always follow up with contacts to (1) find out how your information played out for your contact or (2) tell them how their information played out for you
- Keep contacts alive by touching base with them occasionally
- Think outside the box and be willing to try new things
- Create opportunities not only for yourself but also for others
- Start building your network ASAP!

ENDS AND MEANS

Before you seek out anyone, you need to know three (3) important things:

1. What your goals are
2. What you need to achieve those goals
3. That you're willing to do what's necessary to achieve them.

Your goal's ends and means need to be clearly and carefully defined.

If, like the majority of people, you haven't already determined in detail your ends (goals) and means (methods), make sure that you have committed them to your notebook. Having them in black and white helps clarify your thinking. Furthermore, having them written down gives you a permanent record.

You do *not* want to have to rely upon your memory which can distort your plans and goals over time. This record acts as a guide to which you can refer. You should use this as your "opportunity road map." The sooner you make this assessment the better. You cannot bypass this assessment and expect to do your best.

After you have your goals and how to reach them mapped out, you will discover more about finding the right contacts to match what you need.

EXERCISE 1—Setting Goals

Get your notebook and write down your responses. Begin by looking at both your short- and long-term goals. Ask yourself:

1. What do I want to do or achieve now? That is, of the multiple steps toward my ultimate goal, what will I do first, and second?
2. What do I want to do or achieve in the future? That is, in 5 years? 10 years? What is my ultimate goal?
3. Next, spell out the *whats* and *whens* of those goals in concrete, specific terms. That is, what in particular do I want to achieve when. Be as detailed as possible.
4. Exactly what does my plan generally look like? That is, what is my ultimate goal and what are the necessary steps leading to it?
5. By what date do I want it? That is, what is the deadline for completing (achieving) each step and for achieving your ultimate goal? Be specific about how long it will reasonably take to accomplish the intermediate objectives and final goals

Don't worry that as you gain information and achieve your objectives that particulars in your plan may change. Nothing is set in concrete. You have to remain flexible. You need an initial plan in order to:

- Develop your inner vision of what you want and how you want to get it by identifying short-and long-term goals.

- Design your career development strategies in order to achieve all of your steps (objectives) toward meeting your goal.

- Realize that having your vision means you must follow through on all the steps of your plan.

1. Now go back to question #1 and distill each goal you've listed to a single sentence, or sentence fragment of key words. You want to crystallize it and make it easily remembered.

2. Make a final list of your initial goals, separating them. Then rank them by what you want to do first. Under each goal list the steps (the short-term goals or "objectives") you need to achieve in order to reach that overall goal.

3. Then check it against Joan H.'s Goal Assessment, which follows, asking yourself, How does it match what I've created? What do I need to change? Tweak your list where necessary.

JOAN H.'S GOAL ASSESSMENT

The following table was made out by Joan H., a junior marketing manager with a large business machine manufacturing company, who felt the need to move in her career.

Goal Today's Date: Dec 1	Time Needed	Deadline
Find out about advancement possibilities	1 month	Jan. 1
Let manager know of interest	1 ½ months	Jan. 15
Make manager aware of accomplishments	1 ½ months	Jan. 15
Find career development counseling in company	2 months	Feb. 1
Pursue development plan	8 months	July 1
Make contacts to gather inside info and skills	10 months	Sept. 1
Make move within organization	14 months	Feb. 1

When your goal outline is completed in its preliminary form, you are ready to proceed to the next step: Determining what you need to do to achieve each step(objective) toward your goal.

Remember: A goal is meaningless unless you know what steps you need to take and what resources you need to acquire in order to achieve it.

Look back at Joan H.'s table. Joan's long-term goal is to advance in her career. To her this means concretely and specifically having more authority, responsibility, influence, and money in an area she likes and in which she feels competent. Career development requires that she first figure out what is available to her that potentially meets her desires.

She sees three possibilities, which she ranks as follows:

- Vertical promotion (up a step in her division)
- Lateral promotion (across division lines at the same level)
- Outside vertical promotion (up a step in a new company).

Joan weighs her options and then decides that since she particularly likes her company's environment, she would prefer to stay there. Though lateral promotion would give her experience in other areas, she does not want to become a generalist. She would rather become better at solving problems and managing others in her own specialty.

Having made her decision, Joan starts checking around to see where openings might occur. Further, she checks to see where new positions are likely to be created. Then, with her goals and research data in hand, she goes to her supervisor to express her interest in advancement that fits what is or is likely to be available.

Over a prescribed period of time, Joan reminds decision makers of her goals. In this way she continues to reinforce their awareness of her interest in developing herself. She also demonstrates to them her preparedness to move toward her goals by showing relevant, positive results of her work and how it positively impacts the bottom line. At the same time, she elicits her supervisor's assistance as well as feedback from relevant contacts.

From her preliminary survey and discussions with her supervisor, Joan finds that there is further training that would be useful in a new position: time management and conflict resolution. She goes to the company career counselor to see what she can do to fill these needs.

The human resource development people suggest executive management seminars being held at a local business college. Joan's supervisor approves the expenditure, and she begins. While attending the management program, she tells decision makers of her interest in and preparation for a position she has located within the organization's marketing division.

Remember: Accomplishing your goals means understanding how information works in the marketplace. It means understanding how individuals can be motivated to take the initiative to help you create opportunities for yourself and acting on that understanding.

EXERCISE 2 – Visualizing Goal Achievement

To visualize yourself achieving your goals you need to:

1. First find a comfortable place to sit.
2. Close your eyes and see yourself in the future, in your new position or functioning more fully in your present position.
3. Feel how confident and competent you will be there.
4. Now picture yourself back working on your goal.
5. See yourself actually going through the motions of accomplishing each intermediate step. This means visualizing scenarios within which you are successful and moving forward.
6. With each objective achieved you pat yourself on the back and reward yourself to reinforce that you are making progress.

For example, see yourself finding the seminar you want and attending it. See yourself laying out a career plan and systematically following it. Then see yourself meeting the final objective you set toward your goal. See yourself where you want to be, doing what you want to do, and how you want to do it when you reach your goal.

As you go through this process, actually imagine what it will be like. (*Describe in your notebook.*)

- The challenge
- The accomplishment

Ask yourself what it will mean to you *(Answer the following in your notebook)*

- Satisfaction?

- Power?
- Responsibility?
- Challenge?
- Money?
- Ask yourself how you will feel
- Excited?
- Eager?
- Scared?

Ask yourself the details of when this happens

1. Where, precisely, will you be when it happens?
2. What will you be doing? Describe in detail.
3. How will you feel emotionally and physically at the time? Be specific.
4. Describe your surroundings. See them in Technicolor and vivid detail. See yourself in them. Live each sequence.
5. Repeat your visualization daily. Each time, start the sequence with the next step (objective) and work your way from it to the final goal.

Visualizing your goal achievement makes the process and product, the means and ends, more concrete. You see each step as if it were a small goal in itself. When you see the steps as tangible in your mind's eye, following their sequence becomes easier. Likewise, when you see them as achievable, you heighten your belief in your ability to reach your final goal. Each step achievement is a success in itself. Each step achievement continues to build on that success, aggregating it, making your final goal achievement easier and much more likely.

Repeated visualization of these steps acts as

rehearsal for their actual achievement. You can believe in them and anticipate them because they are becoming more real. Visualization makes the path clearer and reinforces your confidence in yourself that you will achieve that goal.

As the process of visualizing goal achievement becomes more familiar, you feel more comfortable with it. Because it is positive and feels rewarding, it provides an incentive which helps keep you motivated. Visualization creates positive expectations as well as preparation for your achievement. It can help you succeed in achieving each objective and the final goal. You can use this psychological process as well to prepare for networking and any personal relationship goal.

5

SHARPENING YOUR CAREER OPPORTUNITY SKILLS

Of *all* jobs (ranked from highest to lowest), approximately 83% are gotten through contacts. This percentage is even higher at managerial levels and above. In a study of 100 top female executives (vice presidents and presidents) results indicated that nearly 86% of them had had contact relationships which influenced their career development.

HOW AND WHEN TO USE CONTACTS

Once you have your goal and its objectives outlined and your timeline for meeting them assigned, your work really begins: Seeking contacts. By following these simple steps, you will be able successfully to identify and gain access to useful contacts.

Remember: Whether you want technical information, experience, influence, advice, or support, you can get it most effectively through contacts.

To reiterate, a contact is one who informs you, teaches you, develops you, supports you, or guides you. A contact is someone you can meet with and talk to, an individual who is available to listen and give feedback. A contact is someone for whom you can do something and who can do something for you in return.

As you can see, this relationship is a variation on the barter system, one based on fair exchange. There is an underlying assumption of mutuality and reciprocity. Participants in the relationship share. They expect to give as well as receive.

The relationship with a contact may be impersonal or personal, depending upon what the participants want from it. *Impersonal* contacts provide a superficial exchange of information or resources, such as where to find the technical data you want or the right person to see about a job. *Personal* contacts provide hands-on assistance over a period of time, such as helping you improve your problem-solving abilities or grooming you for a new position.

TOM F.'S RESOURCE-SEEKING AND EXCHANGE

Tom F. is aware that his interpersonal skills need help. When his subordinates or colleagues do things he does not like, he boils inside but says nothing. Instead, he lets his anger build up. He feels tense and frustrated. Then, when some trivial incident occurs, he explodes, spewing venom at his confused and humiliated victims.

Tom knows that his behavior antagonizes others. It disrupts the work environment and decreases productivity. He knows that his superiors have heard rumblings of employee discontent and he is concerned.

He also knows that Phil T., a sales manager with his company, had a similar problem handling anger and aggression. Moreover, Phil found help. Even though Tom doesn't know Phil, he seeks him out to find out what worked for him. As a result, Tom gets information and some guidance. Later, Phil asks his new contact, Tom, for his input in another matter, which Tom shares.

You may be saying to yourself, "Sure, you can get some things you want from making contacts, but aren't you really 'using' people to do it?" If you mean "using" in the exploitive sense, the answer is **no**! If, however, you mean "using" in the sense of tapping what is available and/or utilizing what is being offered to you, the answer is **yes**! In this context, "using" is not as accurate and appropriate a description as *sharing.*

Remember: You are not taking away from someone their resources or gifts. You are asking if they are willing to share them with you in an exchange. You give and take. They give and take. They make the decision to do so or not; that is their choice and their responsibility. You are not making them choose to do anything.

If they choose to give to you, it is then up to you to give in return. You can choose to exploit or to share. This is also your choice and your responsibility. But if you choose not to share, you cut off this connection and, perhaps, many others as a result of what is seen as unacceptable behavior.

IMPORTANCE OF CONTACTS

Top executives tend to spend 80% of their time talking with contacts. Moreover, 44% of this verbal give-and-take is with individuals who are outside their organization, specifically with contacts.

Why? Because information from contacts, whether *personal* or *impersonal,* is considered to be inside information, that only insiders have access to. It is considered up to the minute; it has not gotten old sitting on a shelf. It is considered the most reliable because it is most often firsthand.

Contacts have information power. Information power is not having every fact and detail on the tip of your tongue. Instead, information power is knowing where to find the facts and details you want when you want them. Knowing how to make contacts is power. Knowing whom to call is everything.

"The most successful man in life," states Benjamin Disraeli, Nineteenth-Century Prime Minister of England, "is the man who has the best information." (Of course, the same thing can be said for the most successful woman.)

JOAN H.'S CONTACTS

Joan H. perceived networking as a formula: C=I=P (Contacts equal Information equals Power). As a result, she made contacts and sought help from them to develop her opportunities for organizational growth and upward mobility. Through networking, she looked for many people to help her.

Each person she chose provided her with one skill, resource, or type of information she wanted. Her relationship with each of these informational contacts was casual and *impersonal.* They met only occasionally. Joan felt she could get her best advice, support, and power through this type of contact relationship.

The *impersonal* contacts create opportunities, chances, and openings. This fact has been supported repeatedly in research and personal experience. When it comes to creating opportunities or getting a job, the use of contact development, both *impersonal* and *personal,* puts you way ahead of the competition, at the very least getting you an interview if not the job.

EXERCISE 3—Contact Benefits

Take a minute to think about your own experience with contacts.

Ask yourself what are some of the things you have looked for and gotten from others. Be specific what you wanted and for what reason. Write down your answers in your notebook.

- Hints on how to do something?
- Leads on where to find some expertise?
- A single piece of needed information?
- A ready ear for your problem?
- Guidance in learning something new?

You can see that you already have benefitted from contacts.

Now ask yourself what are some of the things you have given to others. You may not even have thought of these actions as "networking." Write down everything you can think of with as much detail as possible.

- Information?
- Emotional support?
- Hints?
- Leads?

- Advice, suggestions, or available options?
- Sponsorship?
- Teaching?
- Development?

No doubt you can see that others have benefitted from you as a contact as well. In the instances you recorded, were you exploitively "using" and "being used"? Or were you "sharing" and "being shared with"? Be as honest with yourself as you can; no one else need read this.

Now ask yourself,

- How did you feel about the process?
- To what degree are you willing to continue to do this?
- What did it mean to you then?
- What does it mean to you now for more formally pursuing your goals?
- How willing are you to making a commitment to "share" resources?

YOURSELF AS A RESOURCE

"Individual self-development in large measure depends upon the focus on contribution," says Peter Drucker in *The Effective Executive.*

For you and others to be useful as a contact, you must first see yourself as a resource. This means that you must be aware of and acknowledge your skills, attributes, abilities, information, experience, and connections. As I have said before, you must see yourself as having strengths that others want and value. You must see yourself as having something to contribute.

You must believe, in your heart of hearts, that you are a unique blend of background, values, knowledge, and work and life experiences. You must believe that you can be valuable to others in an exchange. Very often, people are not aware of the diversity and extent of the skills, abilities, knowledge, and information they have. Unless you make a careful examination, you likewise might be unaware of yourself as a valuable resource.

Thus, in order to achieve greater awareness, it is necessary for you to do an assessment. The following exercise assists you in doing that. Specifically, it helps you determine some of your organizational strengths and areas of expertise, as well as the types of information and experience you possess.

EXERCISE 4 – Strengths You Have

Evaluate yourself in terms of the organizational skills, abilities, attributes, and areas of expertise and information you have. These are some of your most important career-related resources. They can be used by you and others for

- Improving present job performance
- Preparing for career advancement
- Pursuing special interests.

Think carefully about your strengths. Look at the lists of strengths in the accompanying tables. Check under "have" all that apply to you. Add information in the "specify" column that will clarify the "have" and its context.

Now look at the "haves" you have checked. From them list the four (4) items you consider to be your *strongest* in terms of special knowledge and/or experience. These are the *primary* resources that you can offer to others that create your visibility.

Commit these primary resources to a separate sheet of paper, entitle it "My Resources."
Tack up this sheet on a wall in plain view as a constant reminder what you particular want to share.

Having a better sense of yourself prepares you for making contacts. It also bolsters your self-confidence. Why? Because your assessment reveals a basis for self-worth of which you may have been previously unaware, especially if you are reluctant, reticent, shy, self-conscious, or socially anxious.

Visualize this new you. With these strengths in mind see yourself in situations where you used them successfully. This makes you a "recognized expert" of sorts in that strength area. Since this is a role you already hold, and you can see yourself doing it, you know you're not pretending. It's a proven fact. So accept it. The better you can see yourself as a unique resource for others, the more you will believe it, and the better you will project and promote this image to others. Image counts, especially as you promote yourself.

In the following **Assessments #1, #2**, write in your notebook what specific Information/Expertise(s) you've chosen from #1 and what specific Organizational Skills/Abilities you've chosen from #2

ASSESSMENT OF YOURSELF AS A RESOURCE #1:

(Areas of Information and/or Expertise)

HAVE—Specify and Describe

__ 1. accounting, auditing, bookkeeping

__ 2. advertising, public relation

__ 3. agriculture, forestry

__ 4. apparel

__ 5. architecture

__ 6. arts (fine arts, writing, composing music), crafts

__ 7. assessment, testing

__ 8. audiovisual services/products

__ 9. banking, savings and loan

__ 10. beauty services/products

__ 11. broadcasting (cable TV, radio, TV)

__ 12. business development

__ 13. career and placement service

__ 14. computer systems/services/products

__ 15. construction

__ 16. consulting services

__ 17. designing

__ 18. distribution

__ 19. drafting

__ 20. educational and training services

__ 21. engineering

__ 22. entertainment/leisure/recreation

__ 23. exhibitions/conventions/conferences

__ 24. food services/products

__ 25. government (federal/state/local)

__ 26. health care services/products

__ 27. hotels, lodgings

__ 28. interior services/products

__ 29. insurance

__ 30. leasing and rental services

__ 31. legal services

__ 32. manufacturing

__ 33. marketing, marketing research, public relations

__ 34. mining

__ 35. packaging

__ 36. printing, copying

__ 37. publishing, journalism

__ 38. real estate

__ 39. religious services/products

__ 40. research and development

__ 41. sales retail/wholesale, Internet sales

__ 42. secretarial services, administrative assistance

__ 43. social services, therapy, counseling

__ 44. telecommunication services/products

__ 45. transportation

__ 46. travel services

__ 47. utilities

__ 48. website design

__ 49. word processing, freelance and copywriting

__ 50. other

ASSESSMENT OF YOURSELF AS A RESOURCE #2:

(Organizational Skills and Abilities)

HAVE—Specify and Describe

__ 1. organize work to be done

__ 2. identify problems that exist

__ 3. analyze problems

__ 4. establish priorities

__ 5. set clear goals

__ 6. brainstorm solutions to problems
__ 7. evaluate alternatives as solution
__ 8. decide on alternative as solution
__ 9. put decision into effect
__ 10. work with uncertainty
__ 11. improvise
__ 12. foresee consequences of decisions
__ 13. achieve goals despite obstacles
__ 14. delegate responsibility to others
__ 15. find information as needed
__ 16. speak clearly and effectively
__ 17. write clearly and effectively
__ 18. listen, understand what is said
__ 19. state wants reasonably
__ 20. express anger positively
__ 21. relax, reduce tension
__ 22. handle stressful situations calmly
__ 23. accept criticism objectively
__ 24. follow detailed instructions
__ 25. complete tasks on schedule
__ 26. experiment with new ideas
__ 27. instruct, coach, advise others
__ 28. supervise others
__ 29. manage projects and people
__ 30. give orders and stand behind them
__ 31. evaluate others' work/contribution
__ 32. motivate others into action
__ 33. influence and persuade others
__ 34. sell idea to decision makers
__ 35. show understanding to others
__ 36. give support to others

__ 37. put yourself in other's shoes
__ 38. get understanding from others
__ 39. get support from others
__ 40. access others for what you want
__ 41. seek more projects and responsibilities
__ 42. talk with strangers
__ 43. other

EXERCISE 5 – Strengths You Want

You have determined your general goal, step-by-step objectives, time frame, and the resources you can offer others. In order for your contact-making to be effective and efficient, you need now to assess what specific resources you want in order to achieve your goals.

1. You do this by going back to the tables above, called "Assessment of Yourself as a Resource #1, #2," with your WANTS in mind.

2. Go through "Areas of Information/Expertise" and "Organizational Skills/Abilities" and write in your notebook on a separate page every WANT—that's each resource you would find useful to have to achieve your goals.

3. Look at the Wants you have written down. From them make a list the four (4) items you consider to be most important to you for what you want to achieve. These are the primary resources that you want from others in contact exchanges.

4. Put these Wants on a separate piece of paper, entitle it "What I Want," and tack it up in plain view with your list of Haves ... as a constant

reminder.

5. Over time you will fine-tune the focus of your WANTS as you begin to weave the fabric of career opportunity success. Once your desire for achievement is stimulated, your commitment to the goal achievement process becomes more desirable as well.

Remember: In a competitive world, it is even truer that you cannot afford to believe that good things come to those who wait. **They do not!** *You are and have to be the one responsible for going out, looking for career opportunities, and making things happen. It's belief first and then action—lots of action! You absolutely have to establish this new mindset in your career and life.*

You cannot sit back passively. You cannot assume that you will be given the job of a lifetime. You cannot assume that the million-dollar sale or hoped-for-personal relationship will simply drop into your lap.

There is **only one way** that these things will materialize for you. **YOU** have to **MAKE** them materialize.

You have to go out and make the contacts, cultivate them, create visibility and credibility, and use your contacts effectively!

6

PROFITING FROM RISK TAKING

Creating opportunities for yourself requires your making decisions. Decision making, in turn, requires that you make an assessment of the information available, predict outcomes, and take risks.

PREDICTING OUTCOMES
- What are your options?
- What are the *viable* alternatives from which to choose?
- What is the predicted outcome of each alternative that makes it desirable and appropriate, or not?

There are decision-making rules of thumb to help you decide this.

First, when the *problem is simple* and the outcome of each *alternative is known* because information is available (such as when to buy regular office supplies), the *decision is generally routine*. It is often thought of as *standard operating procedure* (SOP). This involves little or *no risk.*

But when the *problem is more complex* but the outcome of each *alternative can be computed* because information is available (such as how much more printer paper to buy for an extra upcoming report), the *decision is straightforward and analytical.* These types of decision making are well-informed, certain, structured, and objective. As such, they involve *little or no risk.*

However, when you are creating opportunities, you often find that you have to make decisions in the absence of complete information. In this situation, it is *not clear what the outcomes* of your possible actions will be. Furthermore, it is likely that each alternative has *several possible outcomes,* not just one.

These decisions will be *subjective* or *judgmental.* Nothing is certain. There is no structure to follow. Moreover, it is not obvious what you have to do to achieve your goal.

You have a *set of choices for actions.* You have *only some information* about the outcomes of those choices. To evaluate and judge the relative merits of the choices available, you must *recognize their limitations.* You then must *establish your preferences* and your *means of dealing with them and their uncertainty.*

All decisions on these choices have varying degrees of risk. The degree of risk depends primarily upon your goal and the environment in which the decision is made. As you go through the rational assessment process, you determine the value of the various alternatives (their perceived contribution) to your goal attainment.

Remember: Since you cannot be sure of the consequences of any given action, you cannot make a perfectly rational decision. And, thus, you realistically must not expect to.

DEALING WITH RISK

First you need to distinguish between alternatives which have acceptable levels of risk and unacceptable levels of risk.

Second, you need to distinguish between real, unacceptable risk and the irrational fear of taking any risk at all. Those who are reluctant, reticent, shy, self-conscious, or socially anxious tend to be uncomfortable with taking any risk.

If fear of risk taking is not a consideration, then you should choose an alternative with which you feel most comfortable. You also choose an alternative that intuitively appears either to maximize, or be "good enough," for your expected outcomes.

The ability to make decisions in the face of uncertainty of outcome is *risk taking*. This ability is a prerequisite for your creating opportunities for yourself. It is important to note that most of the choices you make as you develop yourself are made in the absence of total information. This means that making these choices requires your willingness to assess risk and deal with *real and acceptable risk*.

You cannot be successful in your work or life without taking moderate, calculated risks. In other words, you must be willing to carefully weigh chances and try new things.

Research data support this. In a survey on "What Success Really Means to Me" thousands of high-income respondents reported that there were two important factors influencing their careers: One was "taking risks." The other was "seizing the right opportunities."

CONFRONTING THE UNKNOWN

Since there is no such thing as "riskless development," it is important that you become more comfortable taking risks. However, if you are like a great many people, you may fear doing something new or different, which represents the unknown.

If you fear the unknown, you fear putting yourself in situations which are unfamiliar: Where you do not know the rules, what to expect, and what is expected of you. As a result, you do not know how to prepare for it. In such situations you tend to worry about being embarrassed, failing, and/or being rejected.

The problem is that this reluctance to take risks drastically reduces your awareness of career opportunities. It deep-sixes your decision-making effectiveness. As a consequence, it inhibits your ability to grow, develop, and achieve in both your work and personal life.

"A lot of things that seem like threats can be turned into opportunities," says Professor Kenneth R. MacCrimmons, co-author of *Taking Risks.*

EXERCISE 6—Risk-Taking Assessment

You need to ask yourself, "How willing am I to confront the unknown?" Here are a few questions that may help you answer that question. Test yourself by replying **Yes** or **No.**

- Are you afraid to try a new activity because you cannot do it well? You say, "I don't know what to do so I'll watch." Or you dismiss it by saying, "It's not a very intelligent thing to do anyway"?

- Do you stay with the same old job even though you dislike it, because you feel apprehensive about exploring the unknown of a new job and don't wish to be unemployed at any time if you can help it?
- Do you find yourself unable to change your plan when an interesting alternative comes up, for fear that the new situation will not conform to the way you do things or be as "interesting" as it appeared at first?
- Do you hang around with the same group of friends or associates, and never branch out to become acquainted with new and different people?
- Do you hang back when around strangers or friends because of a fear of what might happen if you started talking?

If you answered **Yes** to any of the above questions, you need to look at your risk-taking behavior. You need to determine your unwillingness or reluctance to take risks. In order to develop your career, you must:

- Surrender the notion that it is better to tolerate the familiar than confront the unknown.
- Allow yourself to be spontaneous and not cling to accustomed, standardized, and unchanging behavior.
- Allow yourself to act independently rather than adhere to what you think is expected of you (by others, society, and yourself).

Repeat the last three bulleted sentences three (3)

times daily, starting with *"I will...."* For example, "I will Surrender the notion that it is better to tolerate the familiar than confront the unknown."

IS PREDICTABILITY SECURITY?

"Not taking risks" means always doing things the same way. It means knowing what is going to happen all the time. However, actually being able to predict what will happen—assuming that non-"psychic" humans could really do that—poses a problem. The problem is that there are no surprises. "No surprises" means no excitement, no challenge, no growth—just sameness.

Perhaps you might like to have a map for your life, a plan you can rigidly adhere to and count on. Prediction would provide you with some semblance of security, like an insurance policy. But, unfortunately for those who desire it, no such plan exists. It cannot exist because it requires that the world outside yourself conform to your wishes. And, like it or not, you have little control over externals, those things that happen outside yourself.

For example, you cannot always control and predict the behavior of others. You cannot ensure the economy will always be favorable to you. You cannot guarantee that you will own the house of your dreams, have the salary you feel you deserve, work at something you find totally satisfying, or find the wonderful personal relationship you desire.

Trying to make the world conform to your expectations of it is an exercise in frustration and futility.

External security is a myth. The only real security

you have is *internal security*. Internal security is your confidence in yourself to adapt, and survive-to-succeed. It is you who chooses and controls what you do. It is you who determines how you respond to events as they occur in the environment. It is you who creates your opportunities. It is you who is primarily responsible for your becoming successful in your career and life.

WHY ARE YOU NOT TAKING RISKS?

Remember: Inability or reluctance to take risks results from some kind of fear. It can be

- Fear of the unknown, where you have a concern for loss of control or predictability of the situation
- Fear of failure, where you have a concern for loss of self-esteem
- Fear of rejection or disapproval, where you have a concern for loss of love or approval
- Fear of success where you worry you won't be able t handle all that goes with being a success.

When you feel fear, you understandably tend to respond by avoiding the thing you fear. If you fear taking risks, you look for old, familiar ways to accomplish your goals rather than attempting new ones. But there are two problems with doing the same old thing.

One is that your standard operating procedure simply will not work all the time. The other is that trying to fit your SOP to each new situation often leads to feelings of dissatisfaction. That is, while you are comfortable with the process (using old means to achieve your new goal), you are uncomfortable with the product (the actual new goal achieved) because it is not exactly what you expected or wanted. It's the result of shoe-horning a size 6 foot into a size 5 shoe.

JACK Z.'S FEAR OF THE UNKNOWN

Jack Z., an engineering manager, looked at all problems as if they could fit into a mathematical formula. He tried to quantify all the variables of a problem. In this way he could structure and easily identify the solution. Jack felt comfortable with this approach and applied it to all situations.

However, while the approach worked with production and engineering problems (where the outcome was certain and objectivity was high), it did not work with personnel or research and development problems (where the outcome was uncertain and subjectivity was high).

Then one day Jack encountered a conflict situation he had to resolve. In order to do so, he had to set up and mediate a negotiation. As usual, he applied his old reliable problem-solving approach. However, when he and the others came away from the bargaining table, there was grumbling and the disquieting feeling among them that everything was wrong.

The process had not worked. Jack had achieved his objective of dealing with the situation. But he had not dealt with it effectively. Furthermore, he had not solved the problem. He had, in effect, only added more layers to it.

What this suggests is that unless he chooses to stretch himself to try new approaches, Jack's inability or reluctance to take risks will lead ultimately to the stagnation of his career and personal life. Even when the amount of risk taking seems small, the benefits derived can be significant.

Robert Frost crystallizes this awareness in his poem *The Road Not Taken*, "Two roads diverged in a wood, and I - I took the one less traveled by, And that has made all the difference."

HOW CAN YOU BECOME A RISK TAKER?

You can become a risk taker by learning risk-taking behaviors. This learning process begins with your awareness that

- Your fear exists
- You can alleviate your fearful thoughts and feelings
- Trying new things can be beneficial.

Your fear of risk taking is an inappropriate, self-defeating, destructive, and upsetting emotion-behavior combination. It arises from the inaccurate statements you make to yourself. What this psychological mouthful means is that your fear is the result of distorted thinking:

- How you think about new situations.
- What you think about taking risks.

In general, your emotional response is the result of a chain of activities you go through when you encounter a situation. Specifically, you:

1. Look at the events and situations which occur in the world. These are, by definition, initially neutral. Then, you as a human being
2. Perceive them (your eyes pass the images to your

brain which records them)

3. Think about the situations and events
4. Interpret them and place your own meanings on them
5. Feel some resulting emotion from this meaning which you then associate with the images.

In other words, how you think about, evaluate, and label the event (as positive or negative) determines how you feel about it and how you are likely to respond to it.

For example, picture this. A young man wearing a clean blue golf shirt and blue jeans, is sitting casually in an easy chair, one leg draped over the arm of the chair. This is a neutral event, with no initial interpretations or evaluation attached, and no emotional response. However, when you attach an interpretation and evaluation, you can watch your response to the situation change.

If you interpreted the scene as the young man relaxing in his dormitory room after a set of grueling mid-year exams, you would probably label his behavior as appropriate to the situation. Thus, you would evaluate his behavior under the circumstances as all right (positive). Your emotional response would follow the evaluation, and you would have good feelings about him (or, at least, not "bad").

If, however, you interpreted the scene as the young man relaxing in the office of the president of IBM during a job interview, you would probably label his behavior as inappropriate to the situation. Thus, you would evaluate his behavior under the circumstances as not all right (negative). Your emotional response would follow the evaluation, and you would probably have bad feelings (or, at least, not "good") about him.

The behavior in both scenarios is the same. The thoughts about it are different. The interpretations are different. The resulting emotional responses are different.

How does this relate to risk taking in general? In order for you to become a risk taker, you need to look at the situation in which your fear occurs

- Look at the thoughts you have attached to the situation
- Analyze how unrealistic they are
- See and acknowledge where lies the distortion: the interpretations, meanings, labels, and evaluations
- Ask yourself about your own fear how likely it is that what you fear would really happen
- Respond to these fear thoughts more rationally and objectively by standing back from their emotion
- Re-evaluate the fear. That is, reinterpret the situation as an opportunity and re-label the emotion positively, like eagerness to solve the problem.

It is absolutely essential that you learn not be afraid to make mistakes. Sandy Weill, former-president of American Express, said, "You must be willing to make mistakes, to make wrong decisions in order to make the right decisions."

You learn from failure because most of your learning from childhood to now has been through trial and error. You learn what has not been working. You learn what has the greater likelihood of working. With mistakes and wrong decisions comes the opportunity for you to find a better way. This is a *key mindset* to how you will develop and grow your career.

Scott Adams, creator of "Dilbert," said, "Creativity is allowing yourself to make mistakes. Art is knowing which ones to keep."

Through assessment of your reluctance to take risks, you can determine both your fear and the underlying thoughts which generate that fear. You can change those underlying thoughts and, thus, change the resulting emotion and behavior. The following is how to do that.

ELIZABETH J.'S FEAR ASSESSMENT

Situation: Elizabeth J. is a pharmaceutical sales representative. She is looking for suggestions on how to sell to a new market. While she is making inquiries of her contacts, she gets a hot lead on the advice she wants. But to get this information she has to pick up the telephone and call a stranger.

Elizabeth assesses her unwillingness to make this call. The following is her assessment (adapted from Dr. David Burns', *Feeling Good*).

Fear Thought: I can't call.
Realistic Assessment. I can call, just pick up the phone and dial. I have the person's name, what she can do for me, and I have a reference.
Thought Origin. (What is there about calling that bothers me?)

Fear Thought: She's busy and does not want me to bother her

Realistic Assessment: She may or may not be busy. Since I am not a mind reader, I have no way of knowing what she will be doing at any given moment. I can't know that she's being bothered unless she says so to me. She might actually enjoy talking with me, taking the opportunity to share. It is her choice how she will respond. I have no right to make that choice for her.

Thought Origin: (If she is busy, why is that a problem for me?)

Fear Thought: I would be rejected.

Realistic Assessment: If she is not interested in talking to me at that moment or does not have the time to talk, it does not mean that she has rejected me personally. She has rejected talking to me at that time. Statistically, I would expect a maximum of half of those people I call to talk to me. That means that half would not.

Thought Origin: (If I am "rejected", why is that a problem for me?)

Fear Thought: I would be shown to be inadequate.

Realistic Assessment: Just because I don't get what I want on one occasion does not mean that I am inadequate as a human being. I am adequate in many things I do. I'm OK whether my behavior works or not at this time. If I see a pattern of behavior not working for me, I can assess and consider changing it.

EXERCISE 7—Your Fear Assessment

In your notebook construct your own Fear-Thought Assessment table.

1. Write down a situation in which you feel a fear of risk taking.
2. Begin by writing down the first fear thought you have when you think of the situation.
3. Then, acting as an objective observer, respond realistically to the thought. Write down your objective response.
4. Now go back to your thought and analyze it: What is the basis of the problem for you?

To become a risk taker you must confront your fear thoughts. First, you counter the automatic thought with a rational response. The fear thought is really a self-criticism, so you have to talk back to your internal critic with a self-defense.

It is often useful to distance yourself from your fear thoughts. This allows you to respond rationally.

1. First, respond as though someone else were objectively presenting the fear to you for analysis. By substituting realistic assessments, you recognize how distorted the fear thoughts are. This helps take the edge off your anxiety.
2. Second, you dissect your fear thought to get to the origin of the fear. Very often the first fear thought is many levels removed from the basic fear thought. Knowing this fundamental fear-generating thought is useful because it can show up in many situations under many guises. When

you know you have a distorted thought and to what that thought is related, you can deal with it and the feelings it generates.

3. Third, you visualize yourself taking the risk you feared. You see yourself surviving and actually feeling good for having confronted the situation.

You know that

- Fear of the unknown, fear of loss or success, and fear of rejection are your own creations
- These fears are the result of distorted and negative thinking
- You can remove the distortion, remove the negativity and think more rationally
- You can recreate your reality
- You can create positive action
- You can create growth.

Peak performers treat stumbling blocks as stepping stones. That is, peak performers treat real failure and rejection as only temporary setbacks. Because you can *choose* how you interpret your world. You can choose to replace fear of risk taking with new, exciting activities to bring satisfaction and pleasure to your career and life.

RECREATING YOUR REALITY

You can recreate your reality by altering the verbal instructions you give yourself when you feel fear. You can train yourself to deal with the fear of risk taking through a simple process: Talking to yourself as you would to a best friend.

EXERCISE 8 – Coping with Fear

Think of a fear situation you experience. You are to
1. Visualize yourself in it
2. Approach this fear situation in your mind
3. Start talking to yourself
4. Prepare yourself for the stress that looms ahead
5. Confront and handle the stressful situation
6. Cope with the feeling of being overwhelmed.
7. Reward yourself for having coped.
8. See, you can be and are your own best friend!

As you go through this sequence, listen carefully to your automatic fear talk then respond with the coping "Fear Defense" self-statements *listed below* and practice them often. You need to apply them every time you approach a risk-taking or fear situation.

FEAR DEFENSE STATEMENTS

You need to *assess* the reality of your fear situation. That is, you need to ask yourself:
- "What is it that really needs to be done?"
- "Is it really dangerous, so I should be afraid?"

You need to *state*: "I will concentrate on what I have to do because that is more constructive than being afraid."

You need to *control* these negative, self-defeating, fear-provoking thoughts and images by saying and thinking:
- "I can erase the worry."
- "Worry isn't helpful."
- "Worry is passive, negative, and not constructive."

Now you need to *re-label* fear by stating: "Maybe the feeling I'm calling "fear" is really a desire to get the situation over with."

You need to *psyche* yourself up to perform well by stating:

- "I know I can confront this situation."
- "I have done this before in X situation and I was successful."
- "I can do it again."
- "One step at a time I'm taking care of it."
- "I am going to think only about what I have to do and stay relevant."
- "I can relax by taking slow, deep abdominal breaths."

You need to *cope* with intense fear by stating:

- "I can focus on what I have to do right now."
- "It cannot and will not last forever."
- "I can wait."
- "I have done it before so I can do it again."
- "I do not have to think about fear."
- "I can do something else."
- "I feel bad only when I think about it."
- "What's the worst thing that can happen?"
- "How likely is it to occur? Not very."
- "Could I cope with it? Yes!"

You need to *positively reinforce* yourself for having coped:

- "I did it."
- "It worked."
- "It wasn't so bad after all."

- "I blew it out of proportion."
- "It wasn't worth the agony."
- "Every day in every way I'm getting better."
- "I'm proud of myself for my continuing progress."

(Adapted from D. Meichenbaum and R. Cameron, in *Self Control.*)

It is important to remember that concentrating on the negative aspects (real or imagined) of a situation promotes negative feelings and lack of growth, whereas concentrating on the positive aspects (real or imagined) promotes positive feelings and growth. You can choose to think rationally, feel positive, and act to reinforce your efforts to create career and life opportunities!

FORMULA FOR RISK-TAKING DECISIONS

Taking risks is not easy, but it is essential to success. It involves knowing what to do and when to do it. Of course, knowing these things is rarely clear-cut. Thus, in order to do it, you need to make your risks more calculated and better grounded. You do this by

- Perceptively assessing the problem situation
- Sizing up the situation
- Recognize the risks involved and what is at stake
- Not prejudging the situation or outcome
- Sweeping aside misconceptions
- Conceptualizing the dimensions of the problem
- Sensing the degree of urgency to solve it
- Assessing the probable consequences of not solving the problem.

To make moderate and calculated risk-taking decisions, you must follow a logical process. This process requires that you (1) ask the right questions and (2) make a rational assessment of the answers before acting.

First, you must recognize that a problem exists. Then you identify it. If it's not Standard Operating Procedure, your problem is a situation for which you do not have a ready and appropriate response or solution. Keep in mind that problems generally carry with them a feeling of discomfort. (You know that feeling in the pit of your stomach that tells you that something needs addressing or is wrong.)

Next you establish objectives. These are the results you want. They are the standards by which you will judge the effectiveness of your decision.

Then you compile a creative and complete list of possible ways to handle the problem. You do this without judging or evaluating them initially. These are your possible alternatives for solutions. They can be applications of existing ideas to the situation to provide the appropriate response. Or they can be applications of a new idea, a new combination of existing ideas, or a combination of new and existing ideas to the situation.

As you look at each of these alternatives to your standard operating procedure, you need to ask yourself five (5) important questions:

1. Does this solution have some lasting value to me or my situation? Is it worth it?
2. Does the solution help me meet my goal either directly or indirectly? Will it further my job or career or relationship?
3. Is the solution an efficient and effective approach?

4. Is the solution necessary and sufficient to achieving my success in general or in a particular situation?

5. How much control can I still exert to achieve what I want if I use this solution? Or does this take the control out of my hands?

As you apply each of the five questions, you now begin your evaluation of the alternatives. You need to evaluate each alternative for its

- Effects (positive, negative, neutral in a particular context)
- Probability of desired/undesired effects
- Seriousness of these effects if they occurred.

Decision making is thinking that results in making a choice among alternative courses of action for a desired result. You make your risk-taking decision by selecting the alternative that offers you the

- Highest probability of working
- Highest desirability
- Highest number of positive outcomes
- Lowest number of negative outcomes.

Many decisions must be made in the absence of complete information. So, as you move through the formula's five questions, be on the lookout for negative responses on your part. These signal your doubt about the appropriateness of the alternative. What you want are alternatives which generate positive responses from you.

Finally, you make a decision by picking an alternative. You put this decision into effect. The decision results in some kind of action. Implementation of the risk-taking solution tells you if this solution will accomplish the goal you want achieved. It also tells you that your desire to achieve your goal is stronger than your fear of taking a risk.

INTUITION IN DECISION MAKING

What have you been taught about what factors make up decision making? If you're like most people, you've been taught that decision making is a strictly rational, logical, systematic process that rejects anything else. Hunches, or intuition, need not apply. Therefore, you do a mathematical cost-benefit and risk analysis. Period.

But, the problem with that approach is that while the logical, systematic, analytical approach is necessary, it is *not* sufficient.

Any time you have to make decisions, you also have an accompanying feeling—sometimes gnawing, sometimes nagging—that something is wrong ... or right ... or still needs to be addressed. It's both physical and cognitive and it's just there. In spite of what you may have always thought, ignoring it is not to your advantage. Why? Because you have that feeling or "sense of something needs to be further considered.

Intuition is a subconscious process that shows up as a feeling. It's not tangible, evident, or deducible. It's your brain telling you that while you've been assessing observables, it has been weighing and calculating un-observables: attitudes, preferences, unconscious perceptions, knowledge of human behavior, and barely remembered relevant experiences.

Intuition materializes in your gut so you'll recognize

it. Once you acknowledge it, you need to accept it as a critical decision-making factor because it is.

Contrary to a common belief, intuition doesn't have a gender. It is not the exclusive domain of women. However, historically women have been socialized and expected to be aware of their feelings, those of others, and others' needs. As such, they are the ones who are generally more schooled in the skills needed to recognize and take advantage of intuition and incorporate it into their decision making.

This does not mean that men don't have intuition. They do. One theory about intuition is that it has broad evolutionary underpinnings. In other words, intuition is a form of emotional radar ... or apprehension. It's like an early-warning system by which you look for and make judgments about signs of threat as well as alert you to positive situations of which you might want to take advantage.

Everyone has the capacity to profit from intuition. But profiting from it requires awareness, honing the ability of intuition, and applying it effectively.

To be a successful self-promoter you need to develop your intuitive skills. You do this by:

- Being aware, observant, and attending to the various aspects of situations, details, and the nonverbal behavior of others
- Storing this information away for future use
- Referring to it for associations, similarities, and relevant emotional and cognitive input
- Combining all these elements to lead you in a given direction.

Studies at Harvard University have demonstrated that everyone makes intuitive judgments in the first 30 seconds of a 15-minute encounter. These judgments are the basis of your first impression. Interestingly, these intuitive judgments tend to have 80 percent accuracy.

But while intuition is essential in decision making, you don't want to use it all by itself or follow it blindly. Like any feeling, it can be influenced by faulty memory, maladaptive thoughts and beliefs, and biases. This is why whenever it's possible to do so, you should combine intuition with the logical, analytical components of decision making. Together they provide you with your most effective decision-making approach.

How can you become more "intuitive"? The next time you experience a hunch, do the following (it only takes a minute or so):

- Examine it carefully
- Ask what specific emotion you're feeling
- Determine the chain of events leading up to it
- Determine what initiated the chain reaction
- Pinpoint specific memories or association which signaled your positive or negative emotion
- Describe what your gut is telling you
- Review the hard evidence which supports your hypothesis to check its validity.

American jurist Oliver Wendell Holmes, Jr., summed it up nicely in 1905 when he wrote: "General propositions do not decide concrete cases. The decision will depend upon a judgment or intuition more subtle than any articulate major premise."

As a person engaged in career development, you must live with risk. But you live with it and handle it intelligently. You do this by good planning, some research, and capitalizing on the ideas and help from others. You get as much information as you can on which to base your decisions. This way you can take risks and survive the process to succeed.

7

MAKE CONTACTS WORK FOR YOU

Networking is still one of the ten major trends continuing to change our lives. Now that you have assessed yourself, you have some sense of what you have to offer in a contact interchange. You also have some sense of what personal obstacles you may have to overcome in order to network. Your next step then, before you network, is to examine who constitutes your own current network of contacts.

Even if you never in the past consciously constructed this network, it evolved all the same. Your existing network, or the circle of people with whom you can get in touch, consists of a primary and a secondary group.

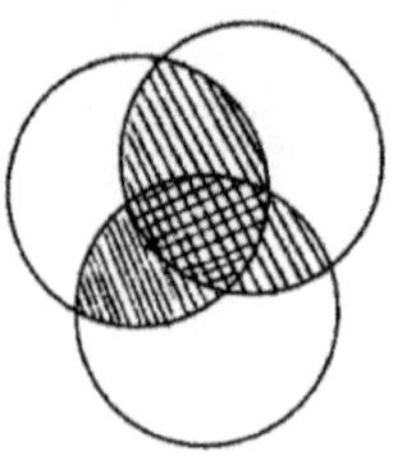

Primary

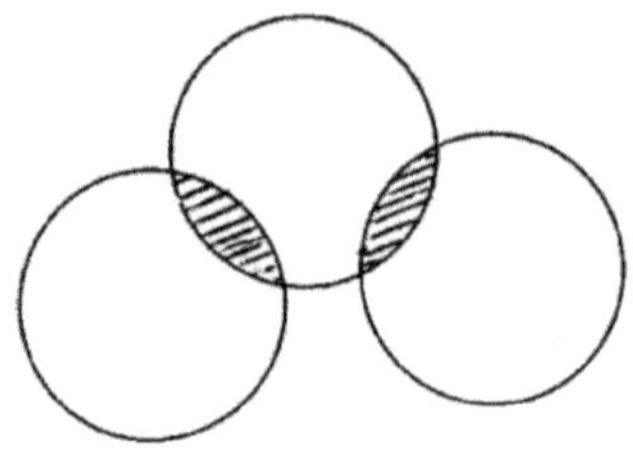

Secondary

Your *primary* group is made up of your family and friends. This group tends to be homogeneous, sharing values, attitudes, beliefs, histories, and friends. Because the members of this group tend to know one another, the network is considered to be closed. Thus, the social circles represented by the members tend to overlap to a great degree. These are your *Personal* contacts:

- Immediate family
- Extended family
- Close friends.

Your *secondary* group is made up of acquaintances and casual contacts. This group tends to be heterogeneous, composed of individuals of different values, attitudes, beliefs, histories, and friends. Because the members of this group tend not to know one another, the network is considered to be open. Thus, the social circles represented by the members tend to overlap very little. These are your *Impersonal* contacts:

- Work, past and present
- Religious
- Civic
- School/Academic
- Organizational
- Associational
- Club
- Professional
- Trade
- Service
- Fraternity or sorority
- Alumni or alumnae
- Volunteer

- Community.

We'll look at the distinction between *personal* and *impersonal* contacts, their applications, and implications a little later. As you will see, both personal and impersonal contacts are important but each has its own context as well as its situational pros and cons.

WHAT IS YOUR NETWORK?

What is the extent of your existing network of contacts? Unless you have focused on the issue before, systematically documenting the contacts you have, you are unlikely to have a clear idea of the number. In fact, you will tend to greatly underestimate it.

The following exercise will help you document the contacts you have. Everyone you know is a potential resource because of who they are, what they do, what they know, whom they know (their contacts), and who knows them.

EXERCISE 9 – Listing Current Contacts

Construct a table in your notebook listing your current contacts—both Personal and Impersonal—using the following list as a guide. Name as many individuals as possible in each of the categories (*not a totally inclusive list*), detailing

1. What they do
2. What you *know* they know
3. Any of their contacts of whom you are aware.

Add additional categories as necessary. Use as many sheets of paper as necessary. Keep adding to these lists

as you remember more people and more categories.
What is Your Existing Network?

- Family (Immediate and Extended as far back as you can go)
- Close Friends
- Neighbors (Past/Present)
- Work Associates (Past/Present)
- Community
- Church, Synagogue, Mosque
- School (Administration, Teachers, Students)
- Organizations/Associations
- Clubs (Social, Hobby, Political)
- Fraternities/Sororities (House parents, Members)
- College Alumni/Alumnae Groups
- Professional Groups
- Trade Groups
- Unions
- Political Groups
- Volunteer Groups
- Medical Service Providers (Doctors, Nurses, Psychological Therapists, Physical Therapists, Dentists, Pharmacist)
- Other Professional Service Providers (Lawyers, Accountants, Insurance Agents, Bankers, Real Estate Agents, Car Dealer)
- Business Service Providers
- State and Community Political Leaders
- Internet Chats, Forums, Groups, Social Media.

Though you may have had some difficulty getting started as you documented your contacts, you probably found it easier as you began remembering more and more people. And very soon the only real problem you encountered was that your pencil could not keep up with your brain as you cranked out names. Chances are that you found you already know a great many people who represent diverse resources—resources which can be useful to you now and in the future.

Job strategist Tom Jackson echoed this sentiment when he said that you are "in the center of a vast information retrieval system which includes virtually everyone at any level who has a connection to your job target field." What he is suggesting is that anyone whom you can contact (by phone, cell phone, text messaging, e-mail, Skype, in person) is a potential source of information and other resources. From them you can even develop good job prospects or other career opportunities.

Once you are aware of your existing network, you need to start cultivating it. Your network is like a field. You need to prepare the soil before you can sow seeds and reap your harvest. To the networker every stranger represents an opportunity, the chance to reach targets, find prospects, and even make friends.

You already know what your goal is. You already know what you need in order to achieve that goal. Now you need to match what you require with what you have determined your network contacts can provide.

Do *not* do it only in your head. Make sure that you do this systematically on paper, in your notebook. Keep a log of what you do:

- Whom you contacted

- What you know about that person
- When it happened
- What transpired
- What you learned or received
- What you will do next.

Then refer to it often!

8

DEVELOPING INTERACTIONAL STRATEGIES

After you have defined your existing network, you need to use it. You do this by following W. Clement Stone's suggestion that you seek advice from those who can help you. "Advice is a commodity others like to share and one seldom in short supply." The challenge you face is in identifying the person who can help you. That person will not necessarily be obvious to you. But finding the right person is important and can make all the difference.

Remember: Where you are tomorrow may well depend upon whom you meet today.

Using your existing network to its best advantage to achieve your goal requires tools. The tools are both attitudinal and behavioral. They represent information-gathering skills. They also represent interactional strategies. The following tools are key to your cultivating contacts, whether they are *personal* or *impersonal.*

COMMITMENT

Your first and most important commitment is to be open to meeting with strangers and making small talk with your goals in mind. (If you have difficulty with small talk, we'll be talking about it in the next chapter.) Since the effective use of contacts requires reciprocity, you need to feel committed to sharing. You need to feel committed to offering your resources in exchange for resources you receive from your contacts. People want to connect and expect to get something, tangible or intangible, for what they give. When the relationship turns out to be one-sided, participants in it become frustrated and uncomfortable. The exchange is inequitable, incomplete, and unsatisfying.

FOCUS

Cultivation of contacts cannot take place until you know what you want to achieve through them. You must acknowledge yourself as a valued resource to others. You must be willing to take risks in order to achieve your goals. You need to determine who constitutes your existing network and whom to approach.

FAMILIARITY

Once you are familiar with your strengths, you want others to be familiar with them also. This means not only potential contacts but also decision makers in your organization (and, perhaps, others). For them to feel the weight and worth of your resources, it is important that you not only perfect your skills but also their value.

Then you must be willing to demonstrate them to others without self-consciousness and excuses. Specifically, when you demonstrate your skills, you must project confidence and competence. Likewise, you need to truly feel comfortable presenting yourself as strong in the areas you let others know you have what may help them solve their problems and you are willing to share it with them.

One useful way to create familiarity is to look for people, places, or events you have in common. You always want to build on commonalities to create bonds. These shared associations attract the other person who already identifies with them and then allows that person to begin to identify with you as well. This is another way you indirectly promote yourself, or "toot your own horn."

But a word of caution is necessary. You have to be willing to deliver what you advertise. It's imperative that you *never* misrepresent yourself with false expertise, experience, or associations. Call is "karma," or whatever you wish, but doing that is nearly guaranteed to come back and hit you like a tsunami of rapidly-spreading rejection. Just the hint that you're not who you claim to be can be lethal to your networking success. In the immortal words of 1970's comedian Flip Wilson's classic character "Geraldine," "Don't write a check with your mouth your body can't cash!"

VISIBILITY

"Seeing what there is to see and being seen for it" is another way to define *visibility*. Being visible requires that you be aware ("seeing") and act on that awareness ("being seen"). In order to cultivate contacts, you need to be visible. To create visibility you first must be alert to which people are more likely to possess the resources you want. Then you must make yourself known to them. Creating visibility, however, should not be restricted to only those about whom you know something of interest.

You must make appoint of meeting strangers and getting their attention. You can get their attention with an "elevator speech." This is a very brief introduction of yourself, stating what you offer, in 20 seconds or 20 words (whichever comes first).

For example, I might say, "I'm Dr. Signe Dayhoff. I turn social anxiety-blocked individuals into confident achievers in only 12 weeks—guaranteed" (17 seconds or 18 words). If prompted to say more, I might add, "Individuals learn how to overcome their fear by eliminating limiting beliefs and maximizing their skills and confidence ... to achieve their personal, social, and work dreams."

You want to make sure you don't give just your name and a job title (like software engineer or coach) because that's not particularly informative or intriguing. It doesn't give the other person much with which to work to extend the conversation. Even saying your name, that you're a coach, and stating the type of coaching you do is better than just your name and occupational label alone. But adding something interesting to that would be a big improvement. A pharmaceutical rep my say with a hint of a smile, "I'm Ann Cloverly and I deal drugs."

Your elevator speech doesn't necessarily come first in the conversation. You might start with a question or statement. But you need to be prepared to state who you are and why you may be of interest when the opportunity arises. Your objective is to start a dialogue so you can learn what others have to offer and how you might be able to help them in exchange.

Questions are particularly useful as long as they are casual and conversational and don't come off sounding like a police grilling. Through your questions you want to learn what their goals are, how well they're accomplishing them, and what problems they may be encountering in the process. You can begin to show them you have resources that may assist them in solving their problem by asking if they've considered an approach in your area of expertise that you think might be helpful. This shows your interest in them as well as what valuable resources you have to offer. If you think they may have resources you'd like to access, you can suggest exchanging resources.

However, not every person you meet will have resources you want. That does *not* mean you don't offer your resources in some form if you can help them with their problem. You want to be as helpful as you can be to members of your network. You are in the process of establishing your visibility and credibility so you help where you can ... without the expectation of immediate or later reciprocity. Being helpful bears rewards of all kinds both sooner and later.

As you can see, like making yourself familiar to others, making yourself visible is an active process. Once you make others familiar with your strengths, you want them to see you often. You want them to associate you with your area of expertise. You want to strengthen this positive association through repetition.

Simultaneously, you want them to think of you as someone interested in helping and have warm feelings about you. In this way, when they think of those strengths and sharing, they will think of you. You never know when someone in your network will discover they have a problem that only you can help them solve. The more people who see you as a resource, a specific and *available* resource, the greater is your contact base—and the greater your opportunities.

If you are in gatherings where name tags are used, use yours. If you imprint your own name on the tag, make it large and legible. Then wear the tag on the right. This placement makes the tag easier to read. The reason is that when you meet and shake hands with an individual, that person turns to the right. A tag on the right is thus closer to their line of vision. As a result, they are more likely to remember it after both hearing and seeing it.

IMAGE

When promoting yourself to achieve visibility, you want to project the image of one who is

- Experienced
- Competent
- Interested
- Giving
- Sincere and authentic
- Trustworthy
- Responsible and dependable
- Involved.

People want to interact with those whom they believe

can provide them with what they want. They want the contact to be open and interested in them. They want the contact to establish rapport and a relationship of some sort with them. Furthermore, they want to feel they can trust that the individual will follow through on promises to them. *They want to know, like, and trust you.* Appropriateness of the impression you create is paramount.

Part of this impression comes from how you behave at gatherings. If wine and cocktails are available, be moderate in your use of them. Overdoing is a double-whammy for you. First, if you are seen to be drinking a lot, you may look as though your confidence and security come out of a bottle. Second, your concentration, memory, trustworthiness, and reliability may be questioned. If, however, you don't drink anything alcoholic, don't make a big deal out of it. Quietly find something else to drink. And if asked about it, smile, and just indicate you'd prefer a soft drink. Then get back to establishing your casual conversation about what the other person does, etc.

If food is available, likewise be moderate. Even if you are starving, do not sit alone feeding your face. People will wonder why you bothered to come if that is what you are going to do. They will wonder if you are there just for the free food. They will question your seriousness. So, you need to find a way to circulate and munch at the same time. If, however, you find that because of your preferences or requirements you don't find anything you can eat, act as though you're not hungry or have just eaten. Whenever possible, let the food and drink add to the sociability of the occasion. And make sure you don't let it interfere with why you're there and what you want to accomplish there.

Presentation of yourself as serious about resource sharing must be consistent from exchange to exchange. When people mention you to others as a possible contact, you want them to have no reservations about your commitment to participate fully in exchanges.

While bragging is not a virtue, neither is being overly humble and modest. Your necessary visibility and credibility do not come from keeping your mouth shut and hiding your talents, abilities, experience, and expertise under a bushel. You *must* create and broadcast the image you want the world to see. You're there to help anyone who needs your specific assistance. You *must* find ways to promote yourself confidently and comfortably.

Remember: You are your own best public relations agent.

ASSERTIVENESS

Cultivating contacts is an active process which, again, means that you do not sit back, waiting for contacts to seek you out. Therefore, when you approach people to introduce yourself to them, you should extend your hand to give them a firm handshake as you pronounce your name, perhaps the name of your company, and what you do briefly, clearly and audibly.

When networking, you need to act like a host, not a guest. It is you who must take the first step. That is, you seek out the contacts yourself. You approach and meet strangers, introduce yourself, and begin small talk. You learn about them then offer to share where and when appropriate. Not everyone is going to have a problem you can help with. But if you know of someone else there who might be able to help, you can bring those two people together.

Assertiveness means knowing you have the right to let others know that

- You are interested in them
- You have something they might want
- You are open to a mutually beneficial exchange.

Assertiveness means pursuing your goal in a reasonable and respectful manner. It also means, however, that others, likewise, have the right to accept or reject your interest. It is important to remember that if an individual rejects your expressed interest in an interaction, 99% of the time that person is rejecting the interchange itself at that time and *not* you personally. This is particularly true in impersonal contact situations.

It's imperative that you not take any "rejection" to heart because you likely have no way of knowing what it really means. Continue to be pleasant and see what happens the next time you meet.

MANAGING YOUR ACTIONS AND TIME

In order to determine and pursue your goals, you must become adept at structuring your actions and time. This means creating a *realistic* To-Do List of the day's proposed activities, ranking all the items to be done. The primary questions to ask yourself are:

- What needs to be done first?
- Second?
- What can wait?
- What can be done by someone else just as well, if not better?
- What do I do that wastes my time without contributing to my effectiveness?
- What can be eliminated altogether?

Having done this, you then must

- Assess how much time each item requires on a regular basis for you to accomplish it.
- Keep a log of your activities and the time involved.
- Work consistently and systematically, day by day, until you achieve the success you want.

In general, it is better to do a little on each item each day than to concentrate your full efforts on Item A on Day 1, Item B on Day 2, and so on. Doing a little of each item each day gets each item closer to completion. It also keeps your stress levels manageable. This necessity for time management applies equally to your career-goal achievement generally as well as your contact making specifically.

Note: While you may pride yourself on being able to juggle many tasks at one time, research has shown repeatedly that *multi-tasking* actually interferes with your focus and concentration. The reason for this is that humans can focus on only one thing at a time. This means that working on more than one task requires alternation from on task to the other.

It then takes the brain about 1.5 seconds to refocus,

thereby, wasting a lot of time and concentration in the switching because you have to get up to speed again. Whenever possible, it is more effective and efficient to focus on one task for a chunk of time (at least 20 minutes) before going to something else. You can accomplish more on each task and the quality of your output will be significantly better.

DEALING WITH DISAPPOINTMENT

There will be times when the results of your best efforts do not meet your expectations. It may be because of faulty judgment or exaggerated hopes. Or it may be totally out of your control. Disappointment can interfere with your confidence. You need to recognize that it can occur, assess why it did, learn from it, and go forward.

WHEN EXPECTATIONS AREN'T MET

How often do you think back about the outcomes you desired but never obtained? Maybe they were trivial or maybe they were momentous. Maybe you expected Ben & Jerry's "Blueberry Cheesecake Frozen Yoghurt" but got "Chunky Monkey." Maybe you expected your marketing tactics for a new product or service would get you greater visibility and credibility, but it never materialized. Maybe the relationship you thought was nearly "perfect" suddenly fizzled.

When those things happened, you likely ran through a progression of emotions (in varying degrees) from sadness to loss to anger to frustration to self-pity. These are the universal components of disappointment.

Disappointment is the result of not having your

positive expectations met. Depending upon the makeup of those expectations, your sense of disappointment may be acute, occurring once or infrequently, or chronic, happening over and over again.

Obviously, not all unmet positive expectations produce disappointment. Those that do tend to result from faulty judgment, unrealistic wishes, exaggerated hopes, or dependence upon chance. The closer your expectations are connected to reality, to the parameters of your preparedness for opportunities when they occur, the more likely your expectations will match the actual probability of what you expect. Reality-connected expectations are significantly less likely to disappoint you, or do so severely.

When you deal with disappointment, it's important to remember that the reasons for your not having reached your goal are, in part, less important than what you thought about it and how you felt about it ahead of time. When anticipating, hoping, wishing, and getting emotionally involved are part of your expectation, they give you a sense of control over the results of that expectation. In fact, the harder you expected it, the surer you were it would happen.

However, when you do this, if it doesn't happen or doesn't happen the way you expected, you will likely feel cheated because of all you have invested emotionally in reaching a positive result.

Disappointment can create a big obstacle to your confidently promoting yourself. This is why clinical psychologist Dr. David Brandt suggests that you think of each of your positive expectations as a continuum of possibilities, ranging from the realistically possible to the realistically impossible.

With respect to dealing with the pain of past disappointments, you need to look at each disappointment like a scientist examining a specimen under a microscope. Carefully you dissect the original expectation by separating out the "wish" part from your belief of the event actually occurring. Then you need to step back to determine how much control or influence you *really* had over the situation.

What you're likely to discover is that there was a lot of magical thinking involved in your expectations. Magical thinking is wishful thinking, a form of self-sabotage which can condemn you to chronic disappointment and hamper your effectiveness and confidence as a self-promoter.

Despite Alexander Pope's writing, "Blessed is the man who expects nothing for he shall never be disappointed," it's imperative that you not chuck your self-promotion, networking, or goal achievement expectations. Achievement expectations are not only important but also absolutely necessary to everything you do. You can't envision seizing opportunities and being successful without them.

The secret to handling disappointment is being pre-emptive. It's making your expectations relevant to your overall goal and the steps leading to it. It's making them

- Positive
- Realistic
- Able to be visualized
- Achievable

- Measurable
- Action-oriented.

But, even the most reality-anchored expectations don't pan out 100% of the time. When they don't,

- Discover what happened
- Learn from what didn't work
- Discover what did work
- Repeat what did work
- Alter your contact-making expectations accordingly.

9

DON'T FORGET ABOUT SMALL TALK

To reiterate, after you introduce yourself to prospective contacts, you need create a conversation in which you can find out if they

- Possess the resources you desire
- Are interested in a mutually beneficial exchange relationship
- Would allow you to contribute your skills to them, their project or organization.

This discovery requires that you encourage other people to talk about themselves, their interests, and their work. This approach suggests the necessity for cultivating the art of *small talk*.

While showing sincere interest in the other person, you want to keep the conversation well directed. As you recall, you are speaking with such individuals in order to find out if they have resources that can help you meet your career-or life related goal. Thus, you want to keep your goal in mind during the conversation but *not* as your *only* focus.

While making an appropriate impression on them, you also want to interest them in you. As a result, you need to carefully tailor what you say about yourself and your goal to them. The problem that may occur is that since you know and have done many, varied things, you're not sure what in particular you want to say to start off the conversation once the preliminaries are out of the way.

When you have a diverse background or interests and experience, you need to ask questions that will provide you with some link that you can follow up on. It's always useful to determine as soon as possible what topics are more likely to create identification. Unfortunately, you cannot always know this ahead of time or discover it as quickly as you like. After you ask your questions to get to initially know this person, you need to listen very carefully to the response. This allows you some latitude in choosing some topic which seems more likely to provide you a direction.

(If you have difficulties with small talk, you can learn how to make through my comprehensive home study e-course, entitled, *How to Speak Without Fear Small Talk Course* at Amazon.)

While you are determining how this person may be of help and you can help in return, you want to consider what you will do next. That is, do you want to pursue a later interaction or end the conversation there and then? The main objective of your conversation is to create a business exchange where appropriate. You can, if you wish, let the conversation digress and become strictly social. That's up to you. However, cultivating business contacts is a time-consuming activity. Therefore, you will want to use your time efficiently and effectively.

Consequently, the conversation need not continue

after you have determined whether or not the contact will be useful. At that point, you can gracefully disengage yourself and initiate a new conversation elsewhere. This is particularly important if you are at any kind of gathering. But just because you're disengaging at the moment doesn't mean you are going to, or have to, let the fire go out. You can take their information and contact them again or even make an arrangement while there to speak again at another time.

However, don't tell people, or let them believe, that you'll call them if you have no true intention to do so. It may seem kind at the moment but it isn't. Furthermore, if you promise to do something for that person, follow through. If they give you a lead, follow up on it, and let them know how it turned out.

If you have not as yet mastered the art of small talk, look for others who have. Those individuals stand out in a crowd. They seem to know everyone. They move about the room confidently greeting people, chatting, introducing one group to another. Observe their behavior and copy it. They are good role models to emulate.

Also, be sure to approach them. Express your sincere admiration for the ease with which they talk with people. If you are not yet comfortable doing this, explain your own initial awkwardness and ask them for a few pointers. This could be one of the best contact moves you make. This is because you are admiring them and asking them to share a little of their expertise with you.

LISTENING

Psychologists have estimated that we spend over 70% of our waking hours communicating. Communication is a shared experience. We listen to understand others' needs. We also listen to influence others.

"Communication is the most important skill in life." – Stephen Covey, author of *The 7 Habits of Highly Effective People.*

Listening and hearing are not the same thing. Hearing is the passive physical process of receiving sound. Listening is the active cognitive process of searching for the meaning of what we hear. Effective listening is not a character trait but a skill that can be (and should be) learned and developed.

Effective (or active) listening is an art unto itself. It requires practice active listening by specifically learning to attend to the three (3) parts of the message:

- Words (data)
- Feeling content (tone)
- Nonverbal behavior (delivery).

Each component communicates important information. Words often do not tell it all.

For example, if Tony W. has been talking animatedly with you about making music videos, the emotional tone of his words suggests his interest in the topic. If Tony then says to you, "Tell me about your experience in making videos," but spends the time while you are talking looking at everyone who passes by, you may feel that he is not really interested in your experience.

His words and nonverbal behavior do not match.

Here the behavior appears to be closer to reality. Nonverbal behavior and feeling content are often a better indicator of the real message than the words alone.

Active listening requires that you check to see that your impression equals the sender's expression. You do this by giving feedback. Giving feedback is reflecting to the sender what you heard being said. Not the words *per se* but what they are intended to mean. Feedback is tangible evidence that you have decoded the message. The sender then confirms the accuracy of your impression, or corrects it.

As you listen actively, you also listen for and note the main points the sender is making. You begin to analyze what is being said. By the time the sender has completed the message, you have thought through the points that have been made and have reached a tentative conclusion. The conclusion is tentative at this point because you still need to see if you received the message accurately.

A most important part of being a good listener is getting the contact's name right, in pronunciation and spelling. I frequently have this problem with other's hearing my name correctly. My name is unusual, but not so difficult that a person actively listening to me cannot get it right. Nonetheless, I preface my introduction of myself with a disclaimer that I have an unusual first name, one not heard often: "Signe." I repeat my first name, emphasizing the pronunciation (sig'nuh).

When a shadow of incomprehension crosses the

other person's face, I now add, "That's *S-I-G-N E* but sounds like the insurance company." In the past listeners would frequently mis-hear and refer to me as Signey, Sydney, Cindy, Digny, Figny, Singe, or Sonya unless I found something with which they could associate the sound.

How did I feel when this happened? The way you likely would have felt. I wondered about the listener's hearing, attention, interest in me, and their level of concentration. I also wondered how useful this person could be to me if they were unable to get my name right. Irrespective of whether any of those thoughts had any reality, they colored my impression of the person.

When there is inattentive listening, the sender and the listener both suffer. The sender feels frustrated at not being heard or remembered as a unique, identifiable individual. The listener benefits less because the sender may be less likely to want to interact under these somewhat distressing circumstances.

However, it is best to always give the other person the benefit of the doubt and, thus, a second chance, since we all can mis-hear and/or make mistakes.

Being a good listener to those in your conversation, or even to those around you, helps you better identify those who can help you. It helps you identify those to whom you can be helpful. What you hear someone else say can be the launching pad to a new conversation. Moreover, being a good listener creates a good impression and a warm fuzziness because everyone wants to believe that others value what they have to say. It creates visibility and credibility for you.

Remember: Being positively remembered is the name of the opportunities' game.

ACTIVE LISTENING

Active Listening is a structured way in which to give individual attention to a speaker. It is done with a genuine effort to understand the speaker's point of view and improve mutual understanding. Specifically, it is listening for meaning then checking with the speaker to see if what you think you heard was received and understood correctly by you. That is, is what you received (heard) congruent with the intended transmission (what the speaker meant by what was said).

To be open to understanding the other person you need to step back from your own frame of reference and suspend your judgment. This is because preconceived notions and assumptions about the other person only muddy the communication waters. As a result, hearing their message accurately becomes difficult.

Checking that the reception equals the transmission reduces the likelihood of conflict. Specifically, where there is an authentic attempt to understand and accept the other person's perspective, there is greater likelihood of consensus, cooperation, and collaboration.

Why is active listening necessary? Too often when we interact with others, we are not fully attentive. We may be distracted, thinking about other things, such as what we want to say—or do—next. When you are not tuned into the same channel as the speaker, you can make erroneous assumptions. You can misinterpret and misunderstand.

Furthermore, the speaker can either consciously or unconsciously sense your disengagement in the conversation. This creates discomfort in the speaker and reduces your opportunity to establish rapport and a trusting relationship with them. Active listening is essential in any good relationship but especially in one in which you are depending upon the other person's assistance to help you achieve your goals.

For listening and responding to be effective, you need to:

- Listen with interest
- Absorb the data content
- Grasp the emotion
- Combine word content and feelings
- Note all subtle nonverbal cues
- Sense underlying meaning of it all
- Respond with behaviors and expressions of attention to indicate you are listening and understanding
- Make no unfounded assumptions about the person's intentions, motivations, or expectations
- Make no unfounded assumptions about what the person means

Remember: When verbal and nonverbal behaviors conflict, go with the nonverbal.

When you listen effectively and respond effectively, you communicate

- I hear what you're saying
- I hear what you're feeling
- I understand how you see things

- I am interested and/or concerned
- I do not judge or evaluate you as a person
- You do not have to be afraid of my censure for speaking out.

The following are your Primary Active Listening Techniques:

Verbal Encouragers include "Yes," "Ah," "Uh-huh," "I see," "Hmm," "Tell me more."

Nonverbal Encouragers include nodding, smiling, using voice inflection and intonation and other body language, such as subtly mirroring the speaker's behaviors.

Reflecting is feeding back to the speaker the *essence* of what is being communicated. However, it is not simply repeating verbatim what was said. If the speaker says, "I don't want to go to work today because I have to give a presentation," a reflective response would be, "It sounds like you're feeling really anxious about the presentation and would prefer to avoid it."

Note: This is tentative since you do not know for sure. You are giving the speaker the opportunity to confirm, reject, or clarify your hypothesis.

Clarifying is taking Reflecting one step further. Clarifying focuses on the key underlying issues and sorting out confusing, conflicting feelings. It's a little deeper than Reflecting, When the speaker says, "I hate this case. Even when I do my best, it's not appreciated," a Clarifying response would be, "It sounds as though you have questions about the value and acceptability of your work in it."

Note: This also is tentative since you do not know for sure. You are giving the speaker the opportunity to confirm, reject, or clarify your hypothesis.

Other responses that prompt Clarification include:

- Tell me more about that

- I'm not sure I understand what you're saying

- Would you ask/state that differently.

Interpreting is offering possible explanations for certain behaviors—as an hypothesis, not a fact. If accurate and well-timed, it can be very useful. For example, you might say, "I've noticed that when you say you want to replace your car, you shake your head. Could this indicate that you really don't want to or have qualms about it?" This observation gives the other person a chance to consider the validity of your hunch and confirm, reject, or clarify.

Other responses that enhance Interpretation include:

- If I understand you correctly, you are asking/stating ___

- You seem to have a ___ (question?)

Questioning is getting you and others in touch with the underlying meaning and feelings. To do this you need to ask "what" and "how" questions. They are open-ended and can be responded to in many ways and, thus, are more informative than closed questions that produce "yes" or "no" answers.

For example, asking, "How do you feel when you get that kind of response from a new acquaintance?" produces more, different, and richer information than asking, "Do you feel burdened (or elated) when you get that kind of response?"

Note: Your asking "why" questions tends to put people on the spot because these questions tend to imply there is likely *one* right "because"-answer that they should know. As a general rule, it is better to avoid "why" questions, using "what," "how," and "to what degree" questions instead.

Other responses that get to the underlying meaning or feelings include:
- What do you mean by that?
- How do you feel about that?
- What are your thoughts on that?
- To what degree do you think/feel that?

Empathizing is sensing the subjective world of the other person and what they are experiencing. If the speaker says, "My weekly schedule is very frustrating," you might respond, "Leaving the house at 6 a.m., traveling all over, then not getting home until 9 p.m. must be exhausting."
Other responses that demonstrate Empathizing include:
- I understand what you're feeling
- I can understand how you might feel that way
- I can see where you are
- I can see how that might be the case
- I'm sure you feel that way.

Confronting is challenging some specific behavior. It is done in such a way that the focus is on the behavior and your feelings about it and *not* on the person who does the behavior. It allows you to share your feelings but helps you avoid evaluating, judging, and labeling the person. When you evaluate, judge, or label, the other person tends to become defensive ... and communication shuts down.

For example, instead of attacking by saying, "There *you* go again, purposely showing how bored *you* are with this," you would say, "When you repeatedly look at your watch and look around the room, it makes me angry because I feel I am not being listened to or treated respectfully."

When you Confront, you need to

- Present data upon which your inferences are based before stating your inference
- Be clear, specific, and concrete
- Present tentatively information that is not fact; present it as an inference
- Use *I-Messages* throughout the confrontation, being careful, caring, and positively constructive

I-Messages communicate the situation from your perspective:

- This is how I see the situation (objective statement of facts)
- This is how I feel (when you do ___, I feel ___)
- This is what I would like to see done as a result (I want you to ___).

It is essential to **AVOID** using *You-Messages* because

they suggest of imply an accusation, criticism, and attack.

Whenever you need to disagree, preface the disagreement with an Empathizing phrase because it shows you are listening and considering what the person is saying:

- I'm sure you feel that way, *but* ...
- I can understand how you might feel that way, *but* ...
- You may be right, *but* ...

Summarizing is crystallizing the statements into a cohesive whole with which you agree or disagree. For example, "It appears that you want to go forward with your promotional campaign for the job at 3M even though you really don't know what the job entails."

WHY IS ALL THIS SO IMPORTANT?

Today more than ever, if you are to achieve your job-, career-, dating, and life goals, you have to interact with others in a relationship-based way. This means you have to be interpersonally savvy and effective. You have to understand that people want to establish connections. It's a form of creating a community and belonging. If they are going to work with you in any way, they want to create a rapport with you and build that into a relationship.

To reiterate: The consequence is that promoting yourself to others and through others requires that they be able to come to know, like, and trust you. You have to come across as sincere and authentic, truly interested in helping others and providing service to them, and not as manipulating or self-centered. Caring and reciprocity are key to making networks work for everyone.

10

HOW TO REDUCE YOUR PROMOTION ANXIETY

Sometimes, even when you have the tools to create opportunities for yourself, you may have difficulty implementing them because of anxiety. You may still feel anxious about approaching the positive goals you are seeking. While this feeling of distress is understandable, it is also controllable. Through the straightforward and easy methods of *anxiety hierarchy* and *abdominal breathing* you can effectively alleviate your anxiety.

Anxiety Hierarchy is a cognitive-behavioral method from Cognitive-Behavioral Therapy (CBT). The procedure is simple, effective, and satisfying. It employs systematic rehearsal of behavior. When you add the physiological relaxation of Abdominal Breathing, you make yourself less sensitive to anxiety-provoking situations.

Since anxiety may be assumed to be a major cause of your inability to approach your goal, Anxiety Hierarchy teaches you to

- Identify the stress thoughts stimulating that anxiety

- Prevent your stress arousal.

(For more anxiety reduction techniques see the new and improved 2nd. Edition of *Diagonally-Parked in a Parallel Universe: Working Through Social Anxiety (2nd. Ed.)* at Amazon http://www.amazon.com/dp/B00BVBOMWO

EXERCISE 10 – Using an Anxiety Hierarchy

Phase One: Think about the stress you experience when cultivating contacts.

- Ask yourself what specifically you find stressful in the process. What elements do you want to de-stress? Write down each element in your notebook, giving a brief description.
- When you have listed all the items in that situation that arouse stress in you, reduce the number to the ten most representative.
- Then arrange those elements as steps in a hierarchy. Rank each element from the weakest anxiety provoker, as 1, to the strongest, as 10.

For example, perhaps your least stressful behavior is "thinking about cultivating contacts" and your most stressful behavior is "speaking to a stranger to gather information."

Here is what your **Anxiety Hierarchy** would look like:

Degree of Stress	Scene Number	Scene Description
Most Stressful	10	Sharing information with a stranger
	9	
	8	
	7	
	6	
	5	
	4	
	3	
	2	
Least Stressful	1	Thinking about networking

Once you have constructed your hierarchy of scenes in your notebook, you will work through it in two (2) ways.

- First you will go through the whole process in your mind. Picturing each scene, feeling the emotion. No thought involved.

- Second you will do it in the real world. Being in each scene, feeling the emotion. No thought involved.

However, *before* you actually start working on experiencing your hierarchy in your mind, you need to implement Phase Two's relaxation techniques.

Phase Two: Since the physiological state of your body has an impact on your neurotransmitters and emotions, you want to approach your stress hierarchy in a relaxed, tension-free state. You can do this by a method called *Abdominal Breathing.*

In Abdominal Breathing your breathing is designed to calm you before, during, and /or after an anxiety-provoking event. It does this both by distracting you from thinking about your body's panic symptoms and by re-balancing your body's oxygen and carbon dioxide balance. Shallow upper-lung breathing which results from anxiety provides too much oxygen to your brain, making you feel dizzy, disoriented, and panicky.

Use the following guidelines for learning and practicing your Abdominal Breathing:

1. Sit in a chair in a quiet room. Place both feet on the floor with one hand on your abdomen and the other on your chest.
2. To the count of five, slowly and gently pull in your abdomen (not tightly) as you exhale through your nose. As you do this your chest should remain as still as possible. Hold this for three counts (Think "1–2–3").
3. Slowly release your belly muscles to the count of five (not moving your chest) and take a small breath.
4. Do not fill up your lungs or breathe so hard that your chest moves. (This constitutes one complete diaphragmatic exhalation-inhalation set.)
5. Continue breathing in this way, counting "1–2–3" each time for ten breaths.

6. Now that you have completed ten breaths, take a moment to see how you feel.

Abdominal Breathing has nothing to do with either deep breathing or shallow breathing. The only determinant of abdominal breathing is that the stomach muscles do the pumping, not the chest muscles.

Every time you need to begin your breathing exercise with an exhalation, never an inhalation. Take small gusts of air. Be careful not to breathe too deeply. If you become short of breath at first, stop and take one large breath. Then resume the slow abdominal breathing. Do this at least three (3) times a day.

Note: When you do abdominal breathing, you are not to be *thinking* about anything. Thinking is distracting. It will negate its physiological and anxiety-reducing effects. When you are going through your Anxiety Hierarchy, you are not thinking about the scene. You are experiencing it. Keeping the process focused on the *emotional* and *physiological* is imperative.

EXERCISE 11 – Further Reducing Anxiety

At other times when you want to reduce stress, you can do *Progressive Relaxation*. Begin by finding a comfortable place and position in which to relax, one with minimum distraction and disturbances. You want to leave your mind blank. Thinking is a distraction. It will make you less able to do the exercise and feel the results. It will also tend to frustrate you which will increase your stress level.

You are going to tighten certain muscle groups and

study the sensations that come from these muscles when they are tense. Then you relax them and notice what happens. (Individuals with physical problems should consult their physicians about doing these exercises.)

1. Start by clenching your right fist while keeping all other muscles of the body relaxed. Study the feeling of tension. Note the location of the muscles when tensed. Hold for about 10 seconds. Then relax the arm totally, letting the tension drain away, leaving the arm feeling heavy with relaxation. Now do the same procedure with your left fist.

2. Work from your hands and forearms to your upper arms, shoulders, upper back and chest, lower back and abdomen and pelvis and buttocks, thighs, lower legs, feet, neck and throat, head and face and eyes and jaw. (Beware of muscle cramps, particularly in legs and feet, when tensing muscles.)

3. In each muscle group concentrate on locating separate muscles. See how many you can find by sensing them. Then tense and relax each. Muscle actions should even include raising eyebrows, wiggling ears, frowning, wrinkling the nose, retracting the upper lip, puckering the mouth, and clenching teeth.

4. When you finish this sequence, consciously relax your whole body, starting at your toes and working your way to the top of your head. Tell yourself, "My muscles are becoming heavy with

relaxation." Visualize each of your muscle groups as white, knotted, and cool. As you further relax them, visualize the muscles as unknotting, becoming smoother. As blood can flow more freely through them, as they relax, you see them becoming redder, warmer, and heavier. See the relaxed muscles as large rubber bands, hanging loosely between bone attachments. See your whole body as limp.

5. To increase your overall feeling of relaxation, start counting backwards from 10 to 1. With each count see yourself as becoming more limp and relaxed. You can continue this stage of relaxation for 10 to 20 minutes or allow yourself simply to go to sleep (when appropriate).

6. When you are ready to rouse yourself, count from 1 to 5. Tell yourself, "At 1, I am waking up, feeling relaxed and alert." At 2, I am more awake and alert but feeling relaxed." Continue to 5 where you tell yourself, "I am totally awake and alert, feeling relaxed and refreshed."

7. Practice this relaxation technique for 30 minutes per day for at least a month to develop the skill.

8. Do this *before* or *after* your Anxiety Hierarchy.

Use ONLY Abdominal Breathing during your Anxiety Hierarchy because there are no cognitive elements which can interfere. You can either tape record a step-by-step description of what you are doing to play back, or memorize the sequence of exercises for daily recall.

PUTTING IT ALL TOGETHER

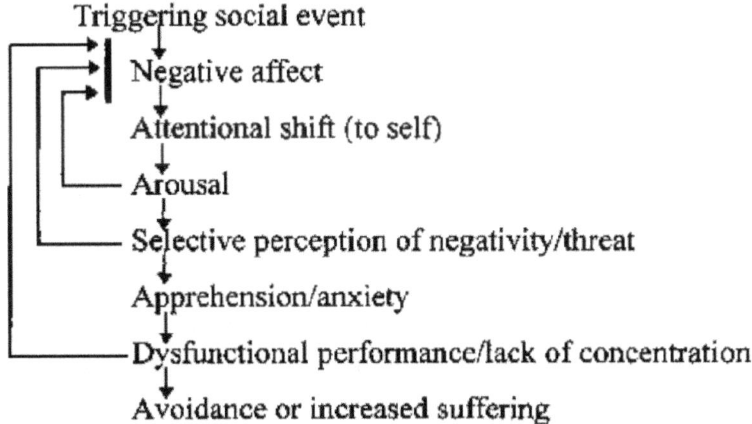

As you can see, anxiety operates on a feedback loop. To reduce your anxiety, you have to interrupt that feedback. You can do it at any stage of the feedback, but as you get better at reduction techniques, you will be able to stop it short closer and closer to the "triggering social event."

Having mastered the total body relaxation technique, you are ready to move to the last phase, Phase Three.

Phase Three: With your body in the final stage of total Progressive Relaxation you need to imagine as vividly as possible the weakest anxiety-provoking scene on your list.

- Look at this anxiety situation in your mind's eye and feel it for 15 seconds.

- If you feel increased anxiety, begin your Abdominal Breathing.

- Stay where you are as you do it. Do not think about anything. Just visualize the scene as you breathe and experience the current anxiety and the reduced anxiety as it lessens. As you breathe, you are allowing your body and emotions to work their way through it.

- When you can visualize the weakest stress scene without any discomfort, you can go on to the next scene in your hierarchy ... and so on.

Go as far as you comfortably can in each session, but do not push yourself. One step per session is usually a good goal. If you feel the abdominal breathing hasn't quite done the job, know that this is natural and expected as you are learning and perfecting the technique. Every time you do it, you will improve.

After you finish each hierarchy session, you can return to Progressive Relaxation if you like. Be sure to congratulate and reward yourself for what you do each time—even though it isn't yet perfect—because each time you're making progress.

By following the steps of your Anxiety Hierarchy you are, in essence, rehearsing how you will feel and behave when you actually encounter the previously stressful contact-making scene. After having ascended the hierarchy in your imagination, you are ready to do the behaviors in real life. Even then, if at any time you feel the slightest twinge of anxiety as you go through the steps, you immediately start your Abdominal Breathing to counter it. Give your body to it without a thought.

Remember: You cannot be anxious and relaxed at the same time.

When your body has a choice, it will prefer a state of relaxation to a state of tension. With the breathing and muscle relaxation skills you have developed, you can control and direct your response to stress. You can then take these techniques "on the road" and use them for any kind of stress and anxiety in any situation. However, be sure to use them at the right time in the sequence: muscle relaxation *before and after* anxiety, and breathing *during*.

11

PROS AND CONS OF PERSONAL CONTACTS

Carl R. Boll, former-Placement Director for Harvard University's Business School Alumni Association, said that in order to take advantage of promotion and executive job opportunities, *personal contacts* are the most effective technique one can use. And, as you have already seen, very few people make their way to the top on their own no matter how bright, savvy, ambitious, or hardworking they may be. Some one person (or many) helped that person in innumerable small and large ways along the line. Even so-called "self-made" people did not do it all alone.

Contact relationships fall along a support continuum, ranging from the Impersonal (peers/networks) on the low end to the Personal (sponsors/mentors) on the high end.

While the end points of this continuum are easy to identify, the roles representing intervening steps are not, such as coach, teacher, or advisor. This is particularly true as the high support end is approached. The labels represent specific behaviors. But, in reality, these behaviors do not occur in isolation. There tends to be overlap.

A person labeled "sponsor" may do more than administratively promote individuals. A person labeled "mentor" may share your career dream with you but act only peripherally for you. Moreover, when these labels are used in common parlance, they tend to be interchangeable, depending upon the speaker's experience and associations.

Someone providing *support* may be called a "teacher," "coach," "developer," "guru," "guide," "counselor," "advisor," "patron," "rabbi," "model," "uncle," "sponsor," or "mentor." Where that supportive contact would be seen on the continuum would be individually determined by the recipient of the support. However, often the terms "sponsor" and "mentor" are used interchangeably, irrespective of what specifically is provided.

Consequently, the type of help you are likely to receive from any contact will likely also falls along a continuum, from data on one end to guidance and support on the other. My research has shown that the contact and assistance scales have certain dimensions that tend to occur together. As already mentioned, information/data functions occur with *impersonal contacts*. Support functions occur with *personal contacts*.

Remember: Because impersonal contacts most effectively provide information and discrete resources and personal contacts most effectively provide counseling, grooming, advice, influence, and continuing support, you need to decide what you need to achieve your goal.

Depending upon what your goal is, impersonal contacts may or may not be able to provide you with everything you want. Likewise, personal contacts then may or may not be able to further provide what you need for your job-and career development and goal achievement. Depending upon your goal, it may be one or the other or, more likely, a combination of both.

WHY HAVE PERSONAL CONTACTS?

Personal-contact relationships are seen as so beneficial that Wheaton College, in Norton, Massachusetts, has helped undergraduates plan their careers through them. In the program, each junior was assigned a personal contact from the college who was working in the student's field of interest. The aim was to (1) ease the transition from college to full-time work, as well as (2) help students assess working conditions in their fields. Wheaton judged over 80% of the pairings to have been successful.

PERSONAL CONTACTS FOR CAREER DEVELOPMENT

The personal contact can function as a career vehicle. That is, the contact can provide you with the exposure, recognition, and visibility needed for advancement. In this capacity, the contact can distinguish you from the crowd of competitors, argue your virtues against those of others, and defend and fight for you in conflict and promotion situations.

If your contacts are persons of influence, they may be in a position to pass on inside information to you.

This may help you bypass hierarchical obstacles, and shortcut cumbersome procedures. In essence, the personal contact puts you on the fast track.

Perhaps more importantly, the personal contact may also generate power for you. Because of the contact's status and your association with the contact, the contact confers different types of power upon you, passing on to you the ability to cause preferred outcomes. As a result, you become personally empowered too.

Power is used here to mean the "ability, capacity, or potential to control, influence, and produce intended effects." This potential is based upon having access to and discretionary use of valued resources. Power is different from control.

Power is the potential to make something happen, like a tightly wound spring. Control is making it happen, like the spring unwinding to ring an alarm clock bell. Your power in the organization exists when a second person, a decision maker, acknowledges that you have this potential. You have control when you are granted the authority to exercise this potential within the organization.

Your contact's resources (special abilities, skills, experience, education, knowledge, information, and network) tend to be transferred to you. Whatever your contact has is perceived as becoming yours through your association with and access to this person. This association with the contact provides a signal to others that you, as a junior organizational person, have influential backing.

When the power, status, and position of the personal contact is reflected onto you, your role in the contact relationship is legitimized.

You are seen to have a wider range of appropriate and acceptable behaviors available to you. Thus, if Lee Iacocca were to have taken you under his wing at Chrysler, your position and actions would have been seen to have a positive sanctioning and legitimizing effect by the organization. In many respects, you could have done no wrong because you were being protected by a powerful other.

INTERPERSONAL BENEFITS OF PERSONAL CONTACTS

The personal contact can also act as an exemplar, a role model with whom to identify within the organization. The contact may be a quasi-parental figure, one whose values, approach, and career moves you can imitate. Most socialization into life and the organization is through role models.

The contact can act as counselor, providing you with emotional support and encouragement, expressing recognition and caring. The contact may guide and instruct you in various aspects of career development. As such, the contact may evolve and function as a friend. In the relationship, you and the contact may interact socially and come to regard one another as confidante or intimate.

Finally, personal contacts may aid you by giving you a sense of competence. They do this by helping clarify your organizational identity and effectiveness in the managerial role. This can help further increase your self-esteem, as well as your credibility.

HARRY R.'S CONTACT PURPOSES

Harry R., like Joan H., is concerned about becoming an endangered job holder. He wants to move up in his production career at the same business equipment manufacturing company that employs Joan H. Because he knows of the many other competent and promising managers with whom he must compete for choice assignments and promotions, Harry also is seeking assistance.

Unlike Joan H., however, he is looking for assistance of a more intimate nature. That is, he wants his relationship with his contacts to be on a close, personal basis. He wants each one of his contacts to provide him with several important functions through frequent meetings. Harry believes he can get his best advice, support, and power through one, maybe two, personal contact relationships.

What Harry wants in a contact is an individual who has access to resources and influence. He wants a person who will take an active and personal interest in him. He wants his contact to act for him in a number of roles over an extended period of time. These roles may include that of teacher, coach, problem solver, model, guide, counselor, developer, friend, mentor, or sponsor.

What is most important to Harry is that the contact (1) make a concerted effort to assist him and (2) ensure allocation of some kind of benefit or reward to him for his work with and for the contact.

ORGANIZATION'S VIEW OF PERSONAL ASSISTANCE

Organizations tend to regard personal contact relationships under the labels of "sponsorship" or "mentoring." Mentoring is the general term for providing some developmental function within a close, personal relationship. Sponsorship, which may occur within mentoring, is the backing by those able to influence the job- or position selection process, either directly or indirectly. To what degree is sponsorship important to opportunity within the organization?

Research has suggested that among those qualified for a position based on ability and past performance, the individual selected is most likely to be one who has the most extensive degree of sponsorship. Even when you add the prized quality of social intelligence to the mix, which is even more important than general intelligence among equally qualified people, where sponsorship is involved, sponsorship will tend to supersede all other qualifications.

Sponsorship or mentoring is generally considered to be an important way by which an organization can assist and develop individuals in the work setting. Having access to such assistance tends to be associated with higher prestige, influence, and organizational status than not having it. Thus, promotions tend to be based on not only ability, performance, and interpersonal skills, but also on degree of sponsorship, recognition, and resultant visibility.

Each promotion you receive is another job assignment which tends to carry with it the expectations of further prospects. Promotion jobs rarely exist in isolation. Rather, they tend to be part of a series of interconnected jobs constituting a "career." Thus, job assignment, gained through contact-generated recognition and visibility, can be considered the single most important variable in career development.

As someone who can manage your political fate in the organization, a good sponsor can provide you with advancement benefits that no one else can or will. For example, they can push through your ideas and projects. That is, they can find and deliver resources for you and authorize budgets and personnel for your projects. By taking your side in hot issues and calming the organizational waters, they can offer you protection. They also can play devil's advocate to strengthen your proposals and act as a sounding board for your developing ideas.

Good sponsors are aware of both how their influence affects the relationship and how this influence is perceived by the organization. As a result, they manage everything having to do with a mentoring relationship in which they're involved. They manage the qualities of their relationship with their subordinates and the perceptions of the relationship by the rest of the organization in order to enhance the effectiveness of all concerned.

DISADVANTAGES OF PERSONAL ASSISTANCE

While personal contacts are generally perceived as positive and beneficial, liabilities do exist. One such cost is dependency. Dependency may exist in your personal relationship if there is a power differential between you and the person on whom you rely for resource. This is frequently the case in organizations.

In a dependency situation you feel obligated to do whatever the contact wants because of what they are doing for you. You acknowledge your dependence on them and allow the contact to influence your behavior. The contact, however, does not necessarily feel equally obligated to you. This dependency makes the relationship unbalanced.

While your dependence may provide you with prime resources, it simultaneously decreases your independence. This means that it could be difficult for you to disengage yourself from the relationship, to assume responsibilities and function autonomously. If within the organization you do not go beyond this personal relationship to expand your power base and expertise, you may remain organizationally static, or, at least, limited in the areas where you can adapt and grow.

A case in point: Sally J. was in quality assurance at Boeing, where she wanted to expand her work boundaries. Sam C. saw Sally's energy, enthusiasm, and desire to grow in the organization and felt he could bring her along. Sam's position in middle management production allowed him to tutor and mold her into what the organization wanted for its management team.

Sally was surprised at how well she responded to his teaching and how well the organization accepted her as an extension of Sam. She felt admiration, gratitude, and respect for him. But she also felt that he was a puppeteer, without whose guidance she would be unable to function on her own in her work.

Personal contacts may also become too invested in you and your dependence on them. This emotional investment parallels that seen in a courtship relationship. Your contact may have difficulty acknowledging, accepting, and dealing with separation as the relationship ends naturally. Excessive investment by either party may result in organizational vulnerability.

With a personal contact you have, in effect, put all your eggs in one basket. As a result, if your personal contact on a project is replaced, you may also be replaced if the two of you are perceived as closely linked. And if your personal contact becomes angry with you, he or she can sabotage your present position or future with the company.

The costs of the relationship may be greater for you than for your contact. This is because you may be perceived by others outside the relationship as being weak, needing a personal contact in order to make it in the organization. The suggestion is that you cannot make it on your own and that you must ingratiate yourself with a powerful, high-status person in order to succeed.

NEGATIVE LABELING

Attributions made to you may be negative. Attribution refers to assignment of causes for events. It refers to how people perceive individuals as being responsible for things that happen to them. To make attributions, people look at actions and their effects which they label as "good" or "bad."

Then they make inferences about the actor's intention to do the act. If the action and its effects are "good" and the actor is perceived as intending them, the actor is labeled as "good." If, however, the action and its effects are "bad" and the actor is perceived as intending them, the actor is "bad."

This attribution process applies to personal contact relationships as well. If you see others having this relationship as negative and that they intended to have it, you will tend to perceive them in negative ways. You will label them negatively.

Research has found that subordinates who did not have personal contacts but wanted them were critical of personal contact relationships, in general, and of others specifically who had them, seeing them as an example of organizational "playing favorites."

OTHERS' PERCEPTIONS OF BEING SPONSORED

My own research on perception of achievement characteristics of young professionals has looked at how others perceive being sponsored. The results support the finding that personal contacts are perceived as important to career development. However, the results also demonstrate that when you have a very visible personal contact relationship, you are perceived by peers in conflicting ways.

In one study, business people acting as company

interviewers assessed job applicants who differed only in whether or not they had a personal contact assisting them in their career. Results of this study showed that study participants evaluated the applicant who had a personal contact relationship as more likely to advance, and more motivated, confident, ambitious, successful, competent, and leader-like. Thus, being assisted by a personal contact can be seen to act as an aid in achieving new roles and meeting role expectations.

In a second study, business students acting as peers assessed the job applicant. While the study participants perceived the applicant as being more likely to advance, they also saw the person as personally being dishonest, unsuccessful, dependent, and lacking leadership qualities.

While both these studies support the finding that having personal contacts is related to the likelihood of advancement, there are differences in how the person with the contact relationship is perceived otherwise. In the study where evaluators were in the role of peer (competitor), they tended to perceive the person with a personal contact personally and negatively because of envy. Where evaluators were in the role of staff (non-competitor), they tended to perceive the person impersonally and positively and see the positive organizational implications of having this relationship.

These studies suggest further that personal contacts are always seen as a vehicle for advancement; but, if you are to benefit from having one, there are specific things you will need to do so as not to be seen as a parasite or incapable of making it on your own. (We'll go into that a little later on.)

INEQUITY

Another cost of a personal contact relationship may be inequity. Equity is an emotional assessment. Each participant expects benefits from the cooperating partner. Each expects what they give to balance what they get. However, if the investments and outcomes do not seem/feel proportional, these expectations may not be met. If equity is not achieved, negative perceptions of inequity tend to result, along with anger and frustration.

A case in point: George A. was being assisted by Jim R. in the finance division at General Motors. Jim had promised George that in exchange for George's heavy research and writing contribution to Jim's monthly financial reports, Jim would make George visible in the division by passing his qualifications on to influential others.

Months went by and none of George's expectations had been met yet. He grew increasingly uncomfortable with his situation. While he saw no visibility for himself, he saw considerable for Jim, who was receiving continual praise for "his" well-done financial reports.

Participants see inequity as a lack of reciprocity. As a result, they tend to feel dissatisfied with the relationship. This feeling of dissatisfaction can be particularly difficult for a person who feels dependent upon the contact relationship.

As you look at the benefits and costs of personal contact assistance, you may be saying, "Sure, personalized help sounds great, but the risks sound great too. I'm not sure I want to take the chance. Too bad there isn't some way I can get the good without all the bad."

Fortunately, you can. You can maximize the advantages and minimize the disadvantages of having personal contact relationships. My research and consulting work with organizations have produced findings which do just that: Help you "get the good without all the bad." These findings, reported in the next chapter, act as guides for your creating your own career opportunities.

12

MAXIMIZING THE USE OF SPECIAL CONTACTS

Through a series of large-scale studies with business people, I looked for and found the conditions which make career development and advancement most likely. Participants in these studies were both male and female who ranged in age from 23 to 59 years. They represented different social, racial, ethnic, and economic backgrounds, as well as diverse work areas. To make the findings useful for application, business people were not asked what they thought they did or might do in a given situation, but were put in that situation to see what they actually did do.

NUMBER AND VISIBILITY OF CONTACTS

While the research indicated that there are two basic ways in which to achieve your success goals, through impersonal contacts or personal contacts, the *number* of *impersonal contacts* and the *visibility* of the *personal contacts* are also important.

Four impersonal contacts are seen as minimum number and essential for providing informational resources. But for these multiple helpers to be most effective in providing their instrumental functions to you, the relationship should have **high-visibility**. This will give you a broad range of information on which to base decisions. Moreover, you will be seen by the organization as having access to diverse information and perspectives.

When you have four who provide instrumentality, such as information in a well-known relationship, you are seen by the organization as a go-getter, successful, effective, productive, upwardly mobile, and a good manager. Your peers also will tend to react positively because if you have four people helping you, it is highly unlikely that each of these helpers sought you out personally to give you their assistance. You must have sought them out. Thus, if you can seek out and get assistance from multiple people, so can others. Having multiple impersonal contacts to provide instrumental functions is a definite plus for your visibility.

One personal contact is seen as maximum number and essential for providing support. But for this single helper to be most effective in providing their socio-emotional functions this relationship should have **low-visibility**. When you have one person who provides stable, ongoing, consistent support in an unknown (known only to superiors) relationship, you are seen by the organization as successful, effective, productive, upwardly mobile, and a good manager.

Having it be unknown to your peers that you have this relationship helps you generally to avoid problems associated with jealousy and perception of favoritism.

While they can still wish they had an influential decision maker to personally assist them, if they don't know about you, they will be unlikely to feel negatively toward you in that respect.

What the findings indicate is that to create the job- and career opportunities you want, you must:

- Create all contact relationships, personal and/or impersonal, as a function of the behavior or resource wanted (yes, you can have BOTH *impersonal* and *personal*)
- Treat all contact relationships, whether impersonal or personal, as business exchanges
- Know which functions (instrumental or supportive) go with which kinds of relationship
- Control the number of your impersonal (4+) and personal (1) contacts who provide you with the specific desired behaviors or resources so you diminish negative reactions and enhance positive reactions
- Control the visibility of your impersonal (increased) and personal (decreased) contact relationships so you diminish negative reactions and enhance positive reactions.

WHAT ABOUT YOUR BOSS AS A SPONSOR?

It is often advantageous to have someone other than your immediate boss in a mentoring or sponsoring role. This is because you and your boss already have a relationship. Your relationship is based on differential power and status. It is not based on an equitable exchange of business functions. If you add to your existing superior-subordinate relationship the element of personal closeness, you create the possibility of even greater vulnerability and dependency for yourself.

With respect to your boss, once again the degree of visibility of your personal contact relationship is important. If that personal contact relationship with someone else in the organization is well-known, your boss likewise may be a concern. Your boss may feel jealous because you are going to someone else for counsel: "Why aren't you coming to me? After all, I'm the one responsible for you." This situation may have unpleasant consequences for both your work and your everyday relationship with your boss. This may apply even when you are receiving your assistance from outside the organization.

Remember: Your career opportunities are the result of the interaction of your behavior and your work environment.

There are many factors which influence the organization's perception of you, factors over which you have varying degrees of control. In order to create the impression of yourself you want, you must control as many of those variables as possible (such as who, what, when, where, and how, and now the degree of visibility of the relationship).

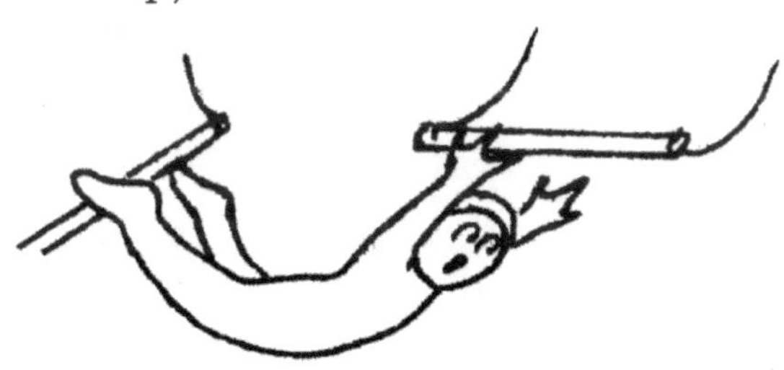

There are many factors which influence the organization's perception of you, factors over which you have varying degrees of control. In order to create the impression that you want, you must control as many of those variables as possible (such as who, what, when, where, and how, and now the degree of visibility of the relationship).

In summary, you must control what you can. That is, you must control, as much as possible, how others perceive you. You do this by knowing how people tend to respond to particular situations. You then maximize the positive aspects of those situations and minimize the negative aspects. This is precisely what you already do, to a degree, by the clothing, hairstyle, accessories you wear, etc. You use these factors and your behavior to create a particular impression of yourself. Positive visibility is key and needs to be striven for whenever possible.

13

HOW TO PURSUE A MENTOR

When you are seeking a specific personal contact for mentoring, you follow the same general procedures you used for seeking general personal contacts. However, the difference is that this time you're not just hoping someone you happen to come across will decide to act as a mentor for you. Instead, when you "pursue a mentor," you have a particular person you want to approach AND you have a structured business exchange in mind for that person.

TAKING CARE OF PRELIMINARIES

In order to pursue a mentor you need to create a crystal-clear image of what you want from that person. Keeping your goals in mind, you search out individuals who appear to have the behaviors or resources you want. When you find people whom you are considering as a personal contact, you disclose to them a great deal about yourself as it pertains to what you're seeking. You communicate your interest in their area of expertise, in what they are doing. In your presentation you communicate to them your own

- Aspirations
- Goals
- Achievements
- Strengths
- Weaknesses
- Risk-taking ability
- Decision-making ability
- Interest in securing assistance.

Your knowing your own strengths and weaknesses tells your potential personal contact that you have done your homework. This demonstrates to them that if they choose to help you, they do not have to start from scratch in evaluating you. Your risk-taking ability is organizationally desirable because it shows your willingness to try new ideas when the standard operating procedure is inadequate.

In this communication you want to emphasize to your potential personal contact that when you are confronted with a novel situation, your fingers will not have to be pried off the procedures manual you have clutched to you heart. Specifically, you are willing to enter new territories, try new things, seek, explore, and discover.

Because risk taking is important in decision making and to your job- and career development, if you are a white-knuckle flyer, you do not want to let it show. You want to find ways to cope with it so you can adapt to whatever the situation may require. If you are still having problems, go back to the techniques in Chapter 5 to alleviate anxiety, fear, and stress, and work on them some more to change your dysfunctional responses to more functional ones.

Employing your coping mechanisms—anxiety hierarchy, fear-thought assessment, fear-defense statements, abdominal breathing, and progressive relaxation—you can learn to de-stress yourself in almost any situation. (I say "almost any situation" because there are some situations in which having a little "stress" can be positive and necessary.)

Remember: Survival and success in both your personal and work worlds are based on learning and applying successful coping techniques which promote confidence.

Once you have identified potential personal contacts and prepared the groundwork for what you want in this relationship, you must

- Assert yourself
- Ask for what you want
- Visualize yourself receiving what you want
- Offer a business exchange.

Offering an exchange relationship increases the likelihood of your receiving mentoring assistance. Specifically, you present the helper with a business proposition. You propose that in exchange for what you want (advice, coaching, or sponsorship) you are willing to share your experience and your abilities with the contact. This says to the contact that you are not looking for handouts. You want an equitable exchange.

Note: You need to keep in mind that you're the one seeking this exchange. You are not being picked for it by someone influential. When you approach someone with the support skills you want, you are presenting them with a business exchange—*a quid pro quo*. This exchange levels the power playing field. It also makes a personal contact relationship less personal.

The general reaction of people to someone who approaches them with an empty hand outstretched is to back away, to run, not walk, to the nearest exit. The general reaction to two hands outstretched, one empty, but the other full (of your resources), is to approach the full hand with curiosity. First, they want to see what they are being offered. Second, they want to see if the right hand balances the left.

WHAT IF THE CONTACT DOESN'T LIKE ME?

Do not be concerned with whether or not the potential personal contact is attracted to you. It is no longer believed that mentoring relationships are based only on interpersonal attraction. While physical attractiveness is a factor in the forming of some social relationships, it has relatively little bearing on the formation of a business exchange.

In a social exchange degree of attractiveness has its greatest impact on initial encounters, wherein individuals are first establishing an awareness of each other. In a business exchange, the initial impact of degree of attractiveness tends to be suppressed or put aside so that the agendas which prompted the encounter can be addressed.

Do not be concerned with whether or not the contact perceives you as similar. Having similar attitudes, values, personalities, social characteristics, or affiliations is not required for having a business exchange. Neither is belonging to the same gender, race, religion, or ethnic background. Your identifying with or having an interest in the potential contact tends to create sufficient similarity between you two to initiate a business discussion.

THE ECONOMICS OF HAVING MENTORS AS CONTACTS

To maximize your benefits and minimize your costs, you must enter into this form of personal contact relationship as equals, each of you giving as well as receiving. Mentoring, when you seek it, is based on this social exchange model. The interaction is regarded as desirable by both participants when the behavior that each produces toward the other is rewarding. This requires you believe that while your respective resources are different, they are of comparable value.

To believe that the mentor's resources are worth more than yours creates a status- or power differential, which, once again, creates dependence in the relationship. You eliminate your dependence on the other person in a relationship so you can become independent and autonomous. This is how you gain more control over your outcomes.

IN PRAISE OF THE ROLE MODEL

Besides seeking instrumental and supportive contacts and mentors, you need to seek out role models. As I am sure you have observed, successful people are exciting to be around. Confident, vibrant with energy, they influence those around them, inspiring them to think with renewed creativity directed toward action. Think of several successful people. Note how their charisma directs and encourages others to want to do more, to stretch the envelope to generate new achievements.

Role models can be helpers too. These are people with whom you can identify. These are people with whom you feel you share something: goals, obstacles, values, or background. These are people who can help you bolster your self-confidence and self-esteem. These are people whose behavior or accomplishments you wish to emulate.

Role models let you know that you are not alone. They demonstrate that others have made it, so there is a chance for you too. They can make all the difference in what goals you set for yourself. Moreover, role models can make all the difference in how successful you are in achieving those goals.

Since men and women, in general, share most organizational skills, individuals entering business and the professions should use both males and females as partial role models. That is, you need to select traits from each that will create for you a composite ideal, the kind of job-seeker or job-holder image to which you aspire.

Role models are important ingredients in the growth and development of your professional identity, vision, focus, and level of commitment.

EXERCISE 12—Finding and Using Role Models

- Make a list of characteristics, attitudes, and behaviors you admire for confidence and success.
- Make a list of individuals whom you admire for their confidence and success.
- Determine what characteristics, attitudes, and/or behaviors they have that help them convey that aura of self-confidence.
- Detail this on paper so you know precisely
- Ask yourself, What specifically do they do?
- Ask yourself, How specifically do they do it?
- Ask yourself, When specifically do they do it?
- Ask yourself, Where specifically do they do it?
- Now take each of those characteristics, attitudes, and behaviors you admire and match it to the behavior of your chosen role models. Then choose three (3) role models to follow.
- Make up a list of the behavioral ways each person demonstrates confidence and success.

In order to try out these behaviors you need to see yourself as this person doing these things and feeling confident.

This means asking yourself what the person thinks, says, and does when he or she does what you want to model. You want to be able to put yourself in their shoes and look at situations from their perspective. To do that you need to decide for yourself

- What that person thinks?
- How do they feel?

- How do they present themselves and their idea?
- What they do to make decisions?
- How they implement those decisions?

Of course, you'll be guessing but the more you can get yourself into their skin the better. You want to see yourself as this person doing these things and feeling confident as a person and as one doing these behaviors.

- From your list of people who do the behaviors you want to take as your own pick three (3) behaviors each day to practice. Review the list three times a day.
- From the list, pick three (3) behaviors each day to practice.
- Then practice those behaviors in front of a mirror, visualizing the person executing them and your matching them. When you feel ready, you will try them out, one-by-one, in social settings.

You practice by being in a social situation wherein you want to act in this desired way.

- You visualize how that role model would look in that situation
- You visualize how that person would act in this situation
- You see yourself in that person's shoes doing the same thing in the same way
- Review the list three times a day.
- Do not forget to reward yourself for each time you do it.

Note: There is nothing phony about doing this. We all do this all the time when we try on new ways to do things. You will be choosing specific behaviors you like to try on for size. You will tailor them to the way you do things so they become yours. You will see what works for you, feels comfortable, and accomplishes your goal.

RENT-A-MENTOR?

Another way to get what you want and be better able to maintain your independence is to hire help. You can offer to pay your personal contact as a consultant. This approach may be particularly appropriate if the contact does not perceive your resources to be useful at that time. Offering payment equalizes the relationship. It shows that you place an economic value on the contact's time and resources.

To do this successfully, remember, it's important for you to have established a relationship with this person first, before you bring up the idea of hiring them. In addition, before you approach this person, you need to have an idea of what a consultant at that level might charge and be prepared to the possibility of having to pay it for this individual's help. When you already have a relationship with this person, your fee for hiring a "mentor" often will not be full price. However, if the contact refuses to take payment, it's necessary to insist on a token payment. Once again, getting the help you need for nothing tends to relegate you to a dependent position.

I witnessed Dr. Clara Mayo (Boston University) and Dr. Jean Griffin (University of Massachusetts) explore this relationship. Griffin, who was in search of further professional growth and development, decided she needed a personal contact relationship. She felt her career was unfocused and unsatisfying. She wanted to learn new skills, refresh old ones, and become acquainted with different professional settings. She decided the paid personal contact relationship would allow her to learn formal skills, goal-achievement processes, and gain information.

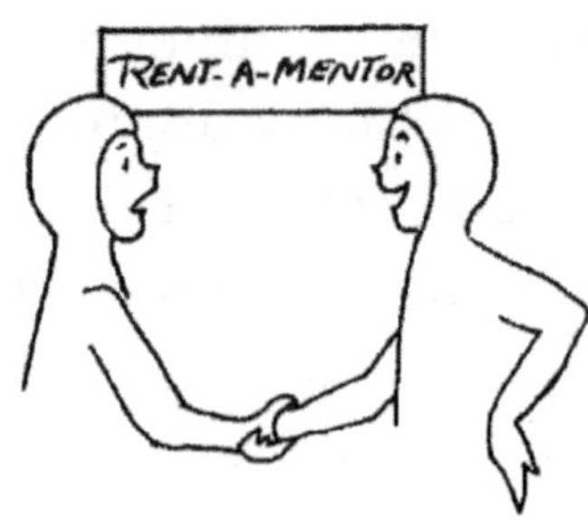

Griffin approached the senior Mayo with a help-for-pay proposition. Mayo, who had 20 years' experience in graduate teaching, was intrigued, so she accepted token payment. She then committed herself to spend two to three hours a week with Griffin. In her role, she evaluated résumés, wrote recommendations, and facilitated Griffin's access to regional networks.

Griffin learned, among other things, how to present papers, how to field questions and handle hecklers. Mayo, in turn, discovered new perspectives on her role in the profession of psychology. She also experienced what she called the "heady feeling of talking with a colleague who is genuinely interested in what I do and how I do it." You can be sure that Dr. Mayo is not alone in valuing that specific result of participating in any kind of mentoring.

OTHER ORGANIZATIONAL CONSIDERATIONS

When you are seeking mentors-to-be within your organization, there are some additional considerations you need to bear in mind. If your goal in finding and cultivating personal helping relationships is to move ahead in the organization, there is certain information you need in order to make your contact choices more effective.

COMPANY PERSPECTIVE

Whether you are working to get a job or a promotion, it is necessary that you discover the top management's perspective. Every company has what is called a "means/end philosophy" that it espouses. McDonald's Corporation, the super-successful hamburger chain, has a simple philosophy: "Fast food, prepared with a consistent standard of quality." This is what the company believes is legitimate, sufficient, and necessary to make a profit.

If, for example, your company believes that it is all right to relax quality control in order to produce more at the same cost, you need to know this. If you are comfortable with this philosophy, you can then look for people who are expert at implementing it.

If not, however, you need to consider if you wish to continue operating within this environment. You should then look for individuals who can offer you some perspective on the situation. They may be able to provide you with:

- Suggestions on how to adapt
- Alternatives to consider

- Expected impact of the organizational philosophy on the behavior of someone who wants to move up in the company.
- Company perspective as applied
- Company history and traditions
- Company size
- Functions of company services
- Company operational and organizational problems.

You see this perspective reflected in:

- Management duties, responsibilities, and authority
- Managers' education and experience
- Company's operating plans and policies.

Gaining access to expertise related only to your job goals is not sufficient to get influential people to notice you. Gaining access to expertise related both to your job *and* the organization's goals is necessary to get those influential people to take note of you. When you move up, you are expected to be more concerned with how your specific tasks serve the organization's general objectives than what you can or will get in return.

HIDDEN AGENDAS

Next it is necessary to determine the hidden agendas in the company. Hidden agendas are the ways that things are actually accomplished within the organization. They are the true operating procedures for dealing with people. You do not find hidden agendas written in the policy and procedures manual. They are not, generally, part of the orientation either.

You learn about them by watching how people, especially managers, behave in the organization. You look for patterns. You ask savvy individuals what these patterns mean to the organization and should mean to you.

One agenda is organizational socialization. It deals with learning the company's expectations of you. Every organizational member is expected to learn the ropes. But how?

Does the company want you to look to your superiors for answers? Or do they want you to look for the answers on your own, in your own way? Do they want you to follow the straight and narrow or explore and test? You need to know this because as you learn your new role in the organization, you establish your place in the company.

This socialization includes learning the company norms, values, and required patterns of behavior. Company norms are the standards by which you are judged: what behavior should be typical for a person in your place. Values are the judgments of goodness or badness assigned to your behavior. The company may expect employees to look to their immediate supervisors for guidance and information. Doing so is valued as good, not doing so is bad.

To get the guidance and information you need, for example, you may be expected to wait until these resources are doled out to you by your supervisor, rather than ask for them when you believe you need them. On the other hand, 3M Company, for example, encourages entrepreneurship by letting various unit operations take the initiative, and not imposing strategies from the top down.

A second agenda is one in which certain individuals and not others are seen as providing the most consistent, stabilizing, and guiding influence at the different stages of the organizational member's career development. If you looked to your supervisor initially to learn the ropes, do you continue to look to your supervisor for what you need? If not, then to whom do you look? This agenda is related to the company's perceptions of usefulness: who is useful to company goal achievement versus who is useful only to your own goal achievement.

The organization's perception of usefulness, in general, is directly related to what produces profit. Those people, positions, and divisions closely linked to the bottom line are seen as having power, prestige, and impact on the running of the organization. These are generally line people, positions, and divisions: such as sales, finance, and marketing. At IBM, for example, the real heroes are considered to be the sales representatives. IBM refers to itself as a "sales-oriented, customer-driven company."

Those people, positions, and divisions who are only

indirectly associated with creating profit are seen as having little or no power, prestige or impact. They provide support and consultation. As such, their usefulness is limited and not as highly valued. These are generally staff people, positions, and divisions: such as human resource development (or personnel), research and development, and consultants.

As a result, if your organization sees staff positions as useful only for increasing what are perceived as secondary skills (interpersonal relations techniques), it would be inadvisable for you to be seen seeking primary skills (decision making, e.g.) guidance from the personnel department. (Unless, of course, you are part of the personnel department and want to develop yourself within that area.)

A third agenda is where to find inside information. Inside information is information that is not available for general consumption. It is privately circulated among selected individuals. It may deal with future plans for the company, upcoming openings, who will be the one to make the decisions on openings, or the existence of important power plays for control at the top.

Getting inside information is based on knowing which grapevines have accurate, reliable, and up-to-date inside information and knowing how to gain access to those grapevines. For example, more business information is exchanged over lunch than at any other time. Knowing who, what, and where is essential because information is power. When you're aware of these agendas, you won't be stuck.

14

CARE AND FEEDING OF CONTACTS

According to Peter Drucker, "Managers have only one tool to effect results … information"

As you collect information, you need to continue to bear in mind that part of the process of taking the initiative in both contact creation and contact cultivation is extending yourself for the other person. Extending yourself is going beyond what is expected of you in a simple exchange.

PROVIDING HELP OR FAVORS KEEPS YOU IN MIND

You want to be aware of the contact as an individual and not just as a resource. Doing this gives you a basis for doing favors, or courtesies, for the contact. These favors let contacts know you are thinking of them in between exchanges of assistance. These courtesies also get contacts thinking about you, which is necessary because it keeps live contacts warm and rekindles cooling ones.

For example, in your conversation with Janet T. you find that she is an amateur nature photographer. She is also especially fond of the work of Ansel Adams. Later, you hear about an upcoming Adams exhibition so you drop Janet a note. In the note, you remind her of your meeting and her expression of interest in Adams. You then mention the details of the showing. The note reinforces your visibility. It predisposes the contact to think well of you and remember you.

If your contacts say they have some information for you or are going to get some for you, do not expect an immediate follow through, or one without a little nudge. Expect instead that you may have to gently prod them.

Follow-up calls or letters sent after a reasonable time are appropriate and in order. Be sure to let contacts know precisely what they promised. Also re-emphasize your eagerness to follow their advice.

GIVING FEEDBACK? ALWAYS!

The care-and-feeding of contacts requires that you always give your contacts feedback. When you are given a tip or help, you must follow through with it in some fashion. That is, you not only do what the contact suggests but also report on progress: initiation, any preliminary results, significant intermediate results, and final results. While this process may seem to be a lot of work, it is not that burdensome. As you will see, a little effort can return a lot of benefit.

Contacts need to know that you value their time, effort, and advice enough to pursue their suggestions. They also want to know how useful a particular piece of information is. Knowing that helps them determine if it is worthwhile to pass on to others. It also tells them how accurate and useful is the source of that information. As a contact, you will need this feedback as well.

Remember: The information provided by contacts usually has been given some thought. Often it has been tailored to meet your specific needs. It is not some triviality tossed your way to placate you. Thus, you need to be careful not to dismiss the help. You should give it the consideration you would want others to give your advice.

Giving feedback to your contacts is an important way to show your appreciation for what they give you. When you are the one sharing your resources, you know how important this is. Think of the times when someone asked you for your advice on their future actions. You went over the situation with the person. You gave it serious thought. And then, you gave them your considered opinion.

Think also of those times when you got no feedback on what happened as a result of your suggestions. Think about how you felt when you did inquire and found that the person had not pursued any of your suggestions. If you are like most people, you probably felt annoyed, a little hurt, and said to yourself, "They didn't even check it out? That's the last time I offer help to them!"

DON'T FORGET DIPLOMACY

If your contact suggests a course of action you have already tried, say that the idea sounds like an interesting possibility. (After all, the idea sounded good to you before you tried it.) Later you report the results. This is courtesy and diplomacy.

If the contact suggests something about which you

have negative feelings, pursue it far enough to get preliminary information. Consider, in view of this new data, if it might be a reasonable thing to do after all. Report on your securing the information and your decision whether or not to pursue. Of course, be diplomatic. You want to be honest, but at the same time you do not want to lose good contacts by appearing to dismiss their suggestions.

If, however, you speak often with a contact (and talk for extended periods of time, discussing a host of ideas), you can readily say, "Yes, that suggestion does sound good. I have tried it, but it does not work that well for this situation."

After a contact gives you a piece of information, gives you support, or promises to pass your name on to an influential person, always do two (2) things:

- Thank the contact. Courtesy is just as important in a business exchange as it is in a social exchange. People just starting to create opportunities for themselves often lose sight of this.

- Follow your expression of gratitude with, "You have been helping me, which I appreciate. How might I give you a hand as well?" Doing this acknowledges that what the contact has done for you is perceived by you as thoughtful and useful.

This reminds the contact that you know that an exchange is in order ... if not now, at least some time in the future. It also gives a feeling of balance. That is, it shifts the focus from your needs, which are being met, to those of the contact, which may not yet have been met. Your redirecting the conversation toward the contact reinforces the bond between you. It shows your concern for the other person's needs. This is a simple investment which costs you nothing, yet pays high dividends.

Important Note: There is an old but true saying that you need to bear in mind. It warns, "If you do something good, three people will hear about it. If you do something bad, ten people will hear about it." This also applies to the goodness of giving feedback as well as the badness of not giving it. All that feedback requires is a telephone call, written note, or e-mail—requiring just a few minutes of your time. In the era of social media good and bad information can be transmitted in an instant and can become viral.

Remember: Your image, your visibility, and your job, career, and relationship opportunities are at stake!

NANCY F.'S FEEDBACK

Nancy F., an organizational consultant, was looking for more work. Elsa D., a public relations contact, told Nancy that she had heard that WalkSoft Shoe Company was expanding and, as a result, needed assistance with its human resource development programs. Elsa said that George B., vice president of personnel and an influential individual, wanted the company to continue its progressive strides in that area.

Nancy did some research on WalkSoft (asked others about the company; looked for articles about it; read its annual report). She then called George B. to discuss the company's expansion plans. When doing so, she made sure she demonstrated her understanding of WalkSoft, past and present. She also described how she had helped companies in similar situations, and thus could be useful to WalkSoft as well at this particular time. After talking with George, Nancy called Elsa to tell her what had happened. Nancy continued to let Elsa know about important developments as they occurred.

A CONSULTANT IS A CONSULTANT IS A...

No matter what you actually do for a living, you should think of yourself as a consultant. You are a consultant because you have experience, expertise, and are an advisor and problem solver. Others come to you to borrow or buy your expertise, inside information, guidance, and support. What you have to offer is a valuable, salable commodity.

You are a consultant for your contacts. Your contacts, likewise, are consultants for you. In order to be effective as a consultant, you need to make yourself more familiar to others. You want them to see you as a recognized expert. You have to market and sell your skills to promote that consultant image.

Rick Frishman, best-selling author of *Networking Magic,* says, "Networking is a matter of helping, sharing, and trusting. It is the most essential, most effective, and least expensive marketing technique available to you as a consultant." (Or as any other worker.)

You cannot succeed without it. Research indicates that consultants are often approached and hired on recommendation. Networking is your primary means of making your skills known to potential clients and other consultants. Networking equals referral where referral is the key to "consulting" success.

BENEFITS OF HAVING CONTACTS

What are some of the things that contacts can do for you or help you do? In your personal life, they can

- Share and help you solve common problems
- Provide emotional support by listening, reflecting thoughts and feelings, and being there
- Help you relieve stress because you have many people to count on
- Enhance your individual growth, expand your horizons, and help you become part of the larger community
- Increase your self-esteem by helping you find that you know more than you previously believed
- Increase your self-esteem by helping you find that you are a unique combination of talents, information, and experiences
- Increase your self-esteem by helping you find that you are needed and wanted for what you have
- Act with others as unified force in accomplishing a common goal
- Present opportunities.

In your work life, by providing advice, support, counsel, sponsorship, and opportunities, they can help you

- Obtain guidance and direction
- Get problem-solving or decision-making instruction or assistance
- Get new business

- Find a job
- Secure advancement
- Market and sell a service or product
- Obtain inside information.

PROOF THAT IT WORKS

There is no doubt that contacts seem useful. However, aside from the anecdotes and stories we all have about contact-generated rewards, are there any controlled research studies supporting their use? The answer is **yes**!

That contacts are useful to you for your career has been demonstrated repeatedly in psychological, sociological, and organizational research over the years. It is not just marketing hype. The following is a classic example, which supports the finding that having access to contacts provides considerable benefits.

For example, in a survey of working men (aged 20 to 60), in largely service- and industry-related jobs, researchers found that job seekers needed two things to reach people of influence: (1) personal resources (most importantly educational and occupational achievements), and (2) contacts. The researchers conservatively estimated that 59% of the respondents had used contacts to get their previous job.

It is important to note that this estimate is conservative in that it reflects the use of contacts *only*. When job seekers used contacts plus other channels, the information was listed as "other channels" and did not reflect the impact of contacts. Most people who use contacts also use other channels.

Having contacts significantly increased these job seekers' ability to reach decision makers. This is important, because getting your foot in the door is half the battle. Moreover, the researchers found that those respondents who said they had gotten their last job through contacts had a mean income that was significantly higher than those not using contacts (varying only by inflation and cost of living). These results suggest that contacts are useful to your career-goal achievement no matter where or when. This is especially true in hard or recovery economic times.

PRACTICE! PRACTICE! PRACTICE!

You need to practice connection-making behaviors often. Practice means:

- Visualizing yourself doing them
- Seeing also what behaviors specifically work for others
- Finally using what works.

While visualization is important for mental preparedness and goal achievement by itself, you also must be with people, and with them frequently, in order to try different contact-making behaviors. This is another place where trial-and-error learning comes in. You must see what works, what suits you specifically, and what seems most appropriate in different situations with different people. The more people and practice the better.

Remember: Emulating what others do does not suggest, however, that you can ignore the various other opportunity-creating recommendations you have received so far and still be effective and successful. What it does suggest is that you can tailor the recommendations (the strategies and tools) and role model behavior to your own style and personality. It is a matter of degree, not omission. You want to use what works best for you as well as for your contacts.

Each of the recommendations is an essential and integral part of the whole method. The more you rehearse your contact-making behavior, the more comfortable and secure you will be with it, and the more comfortable and secure you will be with yourself as you do it.

15

TAKING ADVANTAGE OF OTHER CONTACT RESOURCES

What I often hear initially: "Impersonal contacts sound so cold, while personal contacts sound so warm. Why would I want someone who is detached from me when I could have someone who is attached to me? After all, can't friends do more for you than strangers can?"

These questions are often asked by individuals embarking on the path of creating opportunities for themselves. It reflects the thinking that you can have a good, productive relationship *only* with someone (1) you feel close to, and (2) who likes you as a friend. On the face of it, it indeed might seem that personal contacts would provide everything you need. So why then would you bother with impersonal contacts?

HOW CONTACTS HELP THE JOB CHANGER

Research on what types of contacts provided necessary information to job changers, specifically professional, technical, and managerial found that 16.7% of the job seekers saw their *personal* contacts often, at least twice a week. 55.6% saw their *impersonal* contacts occasionally, more than once a year but less than twice a week. And 27.8% saw their *impersonal* contacts rarely, once a year or less. As you can see, *impersonal* contacts provide upwards of 83.4% of the resources that you need and want when you specifically need and want them.

IMPERSONAL RESOURCES

One reason you want to bother with impersonal resources is practicality. While you certainly get some benefits from personal resources, you do not get all your benefits from them. Moreover, the needs of most workers who want to improve their careers will vary with the situation: that is, their organizational context, personal involvement, and the availability of specific contacts or their functions.

Where personal contacts provide support, impersonal contacts provide instrumentality. What may be seen as a weakness in one type of contact may be a strength in the other. This suggests a *complementarity*. This is the same kind of complementarity that is the basis for the business exchange relationships you create. What both types of contacts can provide, however, is broader perspectives on and more diverse approaches to your decision making at work and in your personal life.

STRENGTH IN NUMBERS

Growing, developing, and achieving your goals requires effective decision making. Successful job holders are those who access the expertise and support they need for decision making.

Ideally, for effective decision making to take place, you should have continuous access to the advice and support of many experienced peers. Those peers should be in noncompetitive businesses and be willing to share their expertise and support. You should meet in a group. You should meet frequently, at regularly scheduled intervals with a structured agenda. It would be especially useful if you could meet under the guidance of a group dynamics specialist, but this may be less likely.

You can increase your decision-making effectiveness and get the best of both worlds through business networking organizations, such as decision-making forums, business lead exchange groups, business roundtables, advisory boards, and so-called "mastermind alliances."

An advisory board is an association of business and professional people who are decision makers from diverse fields. They may meet every other week for continental breakfast, from 7:30 a.m. to 9 a.m., to "network systematically." Each advisory board forum may consist of 12 to 15 members who represent only one firm per industry. This ensures a noncompetitive basis for exchange. Every forum is generally professionally guided for effectiveness and productivity through

- Idea testing
- Problem solving
- Expertise sharing
- Support and identification
- Lead exchange
- Information acquisition.

Participation is expected to be active and interactive. Membership provides peer mentoring in an atmosphere of cooperation, trust, and confidentiality. Not all business networking groups, however, follow this advisory board approach.

Business lead exchange groups (BLEs), for example, systematically regulate what you give and to whom, as well as what you get and from whom. They do this in order to maximize the profitability of each meeting. Specifically, only key sales or management people attend. Each person is often required to bring a minimum of two leads to each meeting. These sales leads can be either for the general group or specific members.

The BLE premise is that networking provides prospects and opportunities for increasing sales and share of market through bona fide leads, because qualified leads and personal referrals are the single best avenue to increased profit. Consequently, BLEs may be less useful for support than for information.

Some business networking groups are small business-oriented. Some are for entrepreneurs. Some are for female business owners. Some are for company executives. Business Network International (BNI) has over 233,000 members in over 8,399 local chapters worldwide. BNI provides a structured and supportive environment of weekly meetings designed to share business, referrals, and establish and develop formal relationships. It claims to be the world's leading "referral organization."

Business networking groups exist all over the

country and represent diverse interests, fields, levels, experience, and goals. They may be free standing or part of the functioning of organizations such as Chambers of Commerce, the Jaycees, and various professional and service associations, like Kiwanis or Rotary, or business and industry trade associations.

Depending upon your own focus and goals, your participation in such organizations can give you increased visibility and access to resources. Investigating what is available in your area is advisable whether or not you choose to become a group member. Check the business section of your paper for a calendar of events. Meeting dates are usually listed, with a number to call for a reservation.

Be sure to ask your contacts for leads to new groups. In many cases, you will be allowed one visit as a guest so that you can get a feel for the group, how it operates, and what it achieves. Be sure to take advantage of the opportunity to visit. Also be sure to create contacts while there.

16

PROMOTING YOURSELF AT WORK

After you have cultivated your existing ties and have accessed new avenues, you will want to keep expanding your circle of contacts everywhere, all the time. New, effective connections can be found nearly anywhere, although some locations may be more immediately profitable than others.

In a study of the top female executives 80% met their most influential helper at work or in a job-related activity. However, 20% met the contact socially, at school or organization, or by chance. This means you must not ignore the vast community around you outside your job or organization.

PROSPECTING AT WORK

Since your most influential helpers will likely be in your organization, let's explore how to make contacts there most efficiently and effectively. (If you are self-employed, you should start with the organizations and individuals with which you do business.) As a reminder, whether company-employed or self-employed, you should approach anyone you feel may be useful because of

- Who they are
- What they do
- Whom they know
- Who knows them.

At work, when should you approach people? A particularly good time in which to approach company associates is during *non*-work moments. Does this mean you can do it only nights and weekends? No. What it does mean is that it is to your advantage to approach a work-related person when they are taking time out, on a break, at lunch, before or after work, at a cocktail party or company picnic, and so forth.

There are several reasons for this. *First*, when a person is at work, there are certain expectations about what that person should be doing. These expectations are held by both the organization and the job holder.

The primary expectation is that the job holder is devoting energy and time to work issues. If you and the potential contact are discussing personal issues on company time, there may be conflicts. These conflicts may be real as well as felt.

There may be some concern about others, especially superiors in the company, learning of this non-work activity, and being displeased. The person approached may feel uncomfortable dealing with a non-company issue on their company time. This will vary among companies, depending upon how rigid or loose they are.

The *second* reason to look for non-work times is related to involvement. Both of you need to be interested and involved in the interaction. If this is not the case, the meeting likely will be a waste of time for both of you.

Aside from having concern about company expectations, the potential contact probably will have many other things in mind at work. It's hard to get helping, sharing, and trusting from contacts or potential contacts when people are distracted.

Approaching a contact at work may make your reasons for making contact seem unimportant and inappropriate. A negative impression may linger. Even if you were to approach this same individual again, this time in a non-work setting, the feelings associated with the first encounter might transfer to the second. As a result, these feelings might bias your contact's response and be less useful to you. While this may not happen, it is safer not to risk it.

In non-work time, the job holder is free to think about and act on non-work issues. Moreover, non-work time, such as company picnics, allows individuals of different power status and job levels to interact as equals. For example, a senior finance person may be uncomfortable if you, a junior finance person, approach during business hours to discuss your personal career goals. However, that same person may feel complimented by your interest and attention if your approach comes after the company softball game, or charity event.

Many large organizations, like AT&T and IBM, have offered formal channels through which their employees can promote themselves, develop contacts, and become visible. Two such avenues are special projects and corporate task forces. A *third* is company bulletin boards and newsletters which identify people from other areas of the company, their interests, and their pet projects.

A *fourth* channel is volunteering for company-wide events. These can be blood drives, charitable events, award dinners, or incentive planning committees. Volunteer work puts individuals from many levels in contact, all working together, in camaraderie, for the same cause. A *fifth* channel is joining or organizing a special interest club.

As you can see, the number of channels open to you in a large organization may be limited only by your imagination. This applies to smaller companies as well.

PROSPECTING WHEN CONDUCTING BUSINESS

Business meetings, particularly if they are cross-organizational, offer opportunities for new connection making. You can address not only those in your company but also those in other companies. While those in your company may be able to provide inside information, socialization, and sponsorship, those on the outside can provide you with diverse perspectives.

BILL R.'S USE OF MEETINGS

Bill R., a software systems designer, is enthusiastic about business meetings. He has found, through his years of experience in the aerospace industry, that business meetings are an excellent place in which to create new connections as well as re-cultivate old ones.

Bill travels around the country. He attends meetings in such places as Seattle, Los Angeles, and Houston. He meets with representatives of organizations such as

NASA and Boeing. He says that while interacting with diverse business acquaintances, old and new friends in these meetings, he has found

- Most of his job opportunities
- New-product information
- New ways of doing things
- New perspectives on how to solve problems
- His best sources of marketing leads.

Remember: In your organization, as elsewhere, you want contacts to lead to positive visibility for you as part of your effective self-promotion. Thus, appropriateness and effectiveness are important elements in making that visibility happen. In this context, you need to be aware of the implications of your behavior.

SKILL OF EMPATHY

There is one behavior that guarantees rewards. That behavior is *empathy*. Empathy is a sensitivity to others thoughts, feelings, attitudes, and behavior as well as the ability to see situations as the other person sees them. This often requires challenging yourself, your attitudes and biases, being curious, asking questions, and leading with your heart, not your head. Learning to be empathetic will always serve you well in your everyday personal and work interactions. But this is especially true in creating new connections and promoting yourself.

17

STALKING THE SOCIAL ANIMAL

There are many locations that can be particularly useful for creating new contacts. Always keep in mind the basic premise of your creating connections: You know that there are people who have what you want, either specifically or generally. You know there are people who can give you what you want, either directly or indirectly. They can be useful because

- They have expertise or experience you want
- They know where you can find facts and leads you need and want
- They have influence to accomplish things for you
- They know and have contact with important and useful others
- Being associated with them also gives you a reflection of their power or influence.

WHERE TO LOOK REMINDER

As we've already discussed, your organization is one. But what are some of the others? One interesting one I referred to earlier was Jerry Rubin's once-upon-a-time Business Networking Salon held periodically at

Manhattan's then-trendy Studio 54 Discotheque. Weekly 2,000 people paid eight dollars to meet, exchange business cards and telephone numbers, and promote themselves.

Other, more commonplace, locations include

- Seminars
- Workshops
- Lectures
- Courses
- Training
- Conferences
- Business meetings
- Stockholders' meetings
- Fund raisers
- PTA meetings
- Professional gatherings
- Associations
- Benefits
- Auctions
- Conventions
- Museums
- Galleries
- Sports events
- Music events
- Trade shows
- Planes
- Church, synagogue, mosque
- Community meetings
- Community events
- Civic activities

- Hobby groups
- Social groups
- Charities
- Retreats
- Chambers of Commerce
- Trade associations
- Business lead groups
- Club meetings
- School reunions
- Alumni or alumnae gatherings
- Support groups
- Chats (online)
- Forums (online)
- Lists (online)
- Bulletin boards (online)
- Political rallies
- Social networking (online e.g., Twitter, Facebook, LinkedIn, YouTube, blogging, etc.)

INTERNET MENTORING AND SOCIAL MEDIA

For those who want the advantages of business networking groups without any of their disadvantages (time commitment, heavy interpersonal interaction, and restrictions on resources exchanged) there is social networking.

What are *social networks*? Social networks are a structure or map of informal relationships between individuals, communities, organizations, et al. They can range from casual acquaintances to family bonds. While business social networks may be particularly helpful to you, you should not ignore the myriad other types of networks available. These can cover almost any topic, for any country or racial group, and can cover subjects as diverse as pop culture, dating, games, music, books, gossip, and languages. For a list of all active social networks with details, you can go online to Wikipedia.

In general, with social networking you may be more likely to find what you want when you want it. You can qualify your contacts initially. The process, which is very structured and systematic, requires less leg work. Furthermore, it can result in access to both impersonal and personal contacts.

However, there are some disadvantages. There is some depersonalization since communication may not be face to face. You have little control over how quickly the contact responds initially and how good the match is. But this is true whether you are waiting for a response on the computer or from a person you have met at a networking event.

If you do choose to become a member of one or more such networking groups—on the Internet or face-to-face, you need to remember that belonging to the group does not negate your need to promote yourself continuously everywhere you can. The group is a means, not an end. If you joined, the group would be, for you, just another resource, another avenue and access to information and to those impersonal and personal contacts.

Ultimately, maximizing your relationship resources will give you a large network of people with whom to exchange information as well as individuals who provide you with personal assistance. It is important to utilize offline as well as online networking. Your contact base is the clay for you to use in locating the potential for creating opportunities. Using your newly acquired development strategies and tools, you mold and sculpt this clay to create your own survival-to-success by opening career and life doors.

SOME LOCATIONS ARE ESPECIALLY USEFUL

Some of these locations are useful in multiple ways. For example, trade shows and conventions provide opportunities for more than making valuable contacts. They offer a chance for you to learn about the guts of your industry. They also offer you a way to broaden your professional perspective. At these functions all aspects of the industry are brought together in one place, from suppliers who serve that business to trade publications describing it.

Each trade show gathering is an excellent learning experience. There is no better forum in which to expand your knowledge of how the business operates. The people you are exposed to there are often the movers and shakers, the ones you should know. They are the ones who make things happen in your industry—and can make them happen for you!

When you attend a function where participants have a common interest or goal, such as a lecture or benefit, you immediately have an established common bond. This bond is something with which you all can identify. Having this bond can be used as an entrée into conversations. It also can be used as a basic relationship link to be strengthened through development.

It is imperative that you be assertive and act on this bond. Your assertiveness in introducing yourself is generally welcomed by the recipient. One reason is that the recipient also may be wading in a sea of strangers and will see your friendly approach as a lifeboat. Your interest and enthusiasm immediately create a good impression, adding to your visibility quotient.

This impression can be enhanced further by your bringing together the various individuals you have met separately. They then become an island of acquaintances. They form, in essence, your own embryonic network. They act as a private rooting section to give you visibility and credibility, thus promoting you.

Research has shown that one important characteristic of self-made millionaires is that they meet as many people as they can. They network everywhere, all the time.

TALK, TALK, AND TALK AGAIN

Wherever you are, it is essential that you talk with as many people as possible. You need to socialize. While doing so, however, you always need to bear in mind

- What your goals are
- What you need to achieve them
- Socializing increases your skills and confidence.

If you know that particular people who are of interest are present, seek them out. You need to make this a **priority** and manage your time accordingly.

Without fail, introduce yourself to the leaders, hosts, and speakers of the function. Do not let their possible celebrity status be a barrier. When you talk with them, let them know of your interest in them and their work. Be sure to disclose something related about yourself. This establishes and enhances your connection.

A case in point: Dr. Robert Chin, internationally known organizational development consultant, psychologist, author, and teacher, conducted a workshop on "Building a Sense of Community in Organizations" which I attended. Dr. Chin's interests and work were very similar to my own, so I talked with him there at length.

I then looked for and created other opportunities for us to become better acquainted. We talked about common issues. This created a bond between us. I offered to help him with a related project he was doing. As a result, when I was looking for an advisor for my doctoral dissertation, an individual I knew was interested in my topic and me, I asked Dr. Chin. Because of his long-standing interest in the subject matter of the thesis and the relationship we had established, he readily accepted the position. For me, the connection proved to be highly successful. For him it was as well because he ended his long tenure at Boston University on a high note.

Michael Levine, a public relations professional, had written a book and was looking for a publisher. But each time he sent out his book outline for consideration, it was rejected. It was rejected, in fact, a total of 100 times!

Levine's response to each rejection was to add the rejecting editor to his network. Within three years a member of his editorial network made a suggestion that led to the book's publication as *The Address Book: How to Reach Anyone Who's Anyone.*

Establishing a connection raises you above the crowd; it creates visibility which is absolutely essential. Once you have established this link, it is important that you indicate your interest in getting together with this person to discuss areas of mutual interest. But, unless the potential contact suggests it, do not try, at that time, to set a specific date for the meeting. Why wait? Failure to get through to people usually comes from doing the right thing at the wrong time.

RECORDING INFORMATION

When you introduce yourself to potential contacts, offer your business card (if you use them). Ask for theirs in return. Every job holder must have cards. This is because cards create an immediate impression, and an immediate impression of you as a professional, no matter what you do. They also provide a convenient way for others to remember and contact you. Thus, cards also contribute to your visibility and credibility.

You can get 100 standard 3.5"x2" business cards for as little as $16, and sometimes less during promotions, from an online printer such as VistaPrint. They also have different sizes, textures, colors, in matte and glossy. It is a very small price to pay for the important recognition.

Use the back of the other person's card to record any relevant information you gather from the conversation. Whatever you think is useful. It can cover:
- Meeting location
- Subjects discussed

- Contact's background and interests
- Contact's abilities and areas of expertise
- Contact's needs and wants
- Networking leads
- Any contact info not on the front of the card
- Appointment date and time.

The data you collect should tell you how you can help the contact and it should tell you also how the contact can help you in return. A small notebook is particularly useful for this for more than very basic information. However, if you are going to do a lot of writing, it is better to make nots now and finish it later, after you finish talking.

Organize this information to keep track of what you want to pursue and what results you have achieved:

- Date the interaction and save the card and information sheet in a card file or notebook.
- Index the contact by the resources offered. This makes retrieving the information faster and easier.
- Keep the file handy, within reach
- Keep it up to date, by interaction, results, and future lines to follow
- Use it often to keep contacts "warm."

As Tony Robbins says, "A life worth living is a life worth recording."

It may be particularly useful to put names, addresses, and all relevant information from contacts in your computer and use some kind of Contact Manager software to organize and access them as well as remind you of times to contact them.

There is no simple formula for networking, contact making, and career success. However, it is increasingly clear that information is a crucial element in your journey to open doors to opportunities and benefit significantly from them.

FOLLOWING UP ON INITIAL CONTACT

Consider, for a moment, the environment of most social functions. In general, social gatherings are hectic. People are milling about, talking, laughing, perhaps eating and drinking. There tends to be little time for each person to do more than touch base with others. Because of the level of distraction, the importance of setting a future meeting date tends to be minimized. On top of everything else, potential contacts are less likely to have their engagement schedule handy in these circumstances.

If you feel these people can be helpful to you in any way, send each one a follow-up e-mail or note. To jog each person's memory, reiterate the circumstances of the meeting. Thank them for your enjoyment of the conversation and/or their participation in the program. Emphasize that you would like to learn more about their areas of expertise or other resources.

Remember: Make the focus on them first and what you can do for them or to assist them with whatever is their interest or pet project, for example.

Be specific. Ask for a lunch engagement or an appointment. If you ask for an appointment, make your purpose crystal clear. Leave no question about your purpose. If you are seeking information about them, make sure they know that that is your real intent—and that it is not seeking a job from them. Then ask for a reasonable amount of time, such as 10 minutes, in which to speak with them. You pick 10 minutes because you want them to know you value their time. They'll choose to extend if they desire to or set up another time with you.

For example, if the contact is a psychologist doing research, know what kind of psychologist the person is (such as, organizational, clinical, experimental, social, or educational, for example). Know what the research is that they are doing (the effect of stress training on managerial advancement, for example). Let them know of your related interest (controlling your own stress in the organization). Tell them what you want to know more about and what you would like to pursue with them. Finally, suggest having lunch on a particular date to discuss this further.

18

OTHER WAYS TO TOOT YOUR OWN HORN

There are many other effective ways to create visibility and credibility for yourself.

SENDING A FAN LETTER

This follow-up note is like a very polished fan letter. By the way, in these hurry-up time, an actual note is more impressive than a dashed off e-mail. In many ways it is similar to a bread-and-butter note sent as a "thank you" after a dinner engagement. It shows your thoughtfulness and interest in the other person. Recipients enjoy the attention. Through this note you are creating more positive visibility as well as developing a rapport. While a physical note is preferable and more personal, an e-mail can do in an emergency situation.

A fan letter can also be directed to those people whose accomplishments you find impressive or whose activities are related to your goals. For example, you read in the newspaper that C. H. has been promoted to general manager at Gamma Globulin, Inc. You read that T. M. has participated in a panel discussion on the use of civil engineering for sports undergarment design. Or you read a letter that R. L. has written to the editor regarding plans for a housing project.

You write directly to C. H., T. M., or R. L. (You sometimes can get addresses from publications; you often can track down these individuals via the telephone book or Internet.) You explain what prompted your letter and why, specifically, you are writing. Whether or not your writing ultimately makes the connection you want, gets you the resources you desire, or accomplishes your goal at that time, your letter is guaranteed to elicit warm feelings and make your name memorable.

"I SHOT AN ARROW INTO THE AIR..."

A case in point: I saw a newspaper article summarizing a panel discussion of management opportunities for engineers. One participant, the director of a college school of management, was quoted as saying that the results of her research were important to those seeking managerial advancement. Her findings indicated that for advancement, method M worked for only situation X, whereas method N worked for only situation Y. Since I was interested in the topic and the director sounded like a good potential contact, I wrote to her. Specifically, I wrote that I

- Had read her quote in the *Boston Globe*
- Found her results interesting but that my research indicated that methods M and N could work in both situations X and Y
- Wanted to know more about her research
- Was interested in discussing the topic in general

to learn of her experiences

- Wanted to get together the following week, if possible, for lunch to discuss how we might benefit one another.

The director's response to my note was an immediate telephone call. She told me that she had been misquoted in the paper. In fact, her research findings paralleled mine. She, likewise, was interested in what other research in that area indicated. I asked what she was doing currently in that area; then I disclosed what I was doing.

She said she was engaged in a project with a national organization which, based upon what I said, she believed could use my experience. The upshot was that within a week, I had met with both her and the national non-profit's representative. Moreover, I was hired as their project consultant.

This example is not to suggest that all contacts produce immediate or immediately useful results. It is to suggest that contacts can come from anywhere. You, however, **have to be alert** to what is around you. You have to use your imagination. You have to be willing to go after what you want but be willing to be available to help first. Finally, you have to take action.

Success depends upon your generating in yourself the sustaining qualities of

- Openness
- Positive attitude
- Enthusiasm
- Self-awareness
- Listening

- Motivation
- Determination
- Problem solving
- Risk taking
- Reserving judgment
- Preparation.

American Connector Expert, Larry Benet is an excellent example of how to make connections, create visibility, and open doors to opportunities. He can meet and get to know nearly anyone. As a result of his skills, he works with worthy charities and non-profit causes around the world to raise millions of dollars to help them. He has worked with Larry King, Richard Branson, and Nelson Mandela, to name only a very few of his vast acquaintanceship with celebrities and the powerful.

One story Benet tells is when he was staying at the Bellagio in Las Vegas and wanted to use their gym very early in the morning. When it wasn't as yet open, he spoke with an employee about what the hotel had to offer if he were to have his next event there. The person, named Marilyn, provided him with great information. As a result, he asked for her name and the name of the Bellagio's CEO so he could send a note about how helpful she had been.

Just then a man walked toward the gym. Benet called him over and praised Marilyn to him. The entered the gym together. As Benet later found out, the man was the Bellagio's COO, Jim Murren. A week later Benet received a note from Marilyn, asking him to visit again.

CREATIVELY TOOTING YOUR OWN HORN

Another way you prepare the groundwork for creating connections is by announcing to the world, not just to individuals, that you exist and have certain valuable resources to offer. There are a number of ways to do this. You can, for example,

- Tell everyone you know you are looking for a particular kind of job
- Give an informal or formal talk, speech, or lecture
- Conduct a discussion, class, seminar, or workshop
- Make sure that any presentation be announced in media
- Be on a panel
- Create a MasterMind group
- Create networking group and announce meetings
- Ask influential others to speak to your group
- Interview influential people and write article
- Speak up on conference calls
- Create your own teleseminar or conference call
- Record your speeches, teleseminars, or interviews and give them away as MP3 or CD
- Speak to an issue at an association, organization, Chamber, or town meeting
- Write an article for a local newspaper, newsletter, or regional magazine
- Write a column for a local paper with useful tips
- Create an e-zine or blog with weekly or bi-weekly posts
- Make blog posts available for iPods
- Create a 2-3-minute video for YouTube on your topic

- Makes copies of published articles to give away
- Create booklet of your collected tips to give away
- Make booklets available in bulk to companies of interest
- Do a survey on topic and report results to media, in e-zine, on a blog
- Do survey, asking for most burning question on particular topic
- Offer to be interviewed for a timely article
- Offer to be interviewed on a teleseminar
- Offer to be interviewed on radio and/or television
- Have video or audio copies made of the interview to share
- Write letters to the editors of magazines and papers on topical issues to which your strengths (experience, information, and expertise) apply.

If this is a totally new experience for you, start small and ease yourself into it. Get help from someone who has already done any of these promotional methods. If you don't know someone, ask a contact and/or get on a list for publicity or PR people. As you gain practice and confidence, widen your scope. In doing these things, you are making yourself available for others to contact you.

One advantage of this approach is that you reach larger numbers of people, potential contacts, per hour of your time. Think of how many people will read a published letter to the editor in your Sunday newspaper. Half the paper's readers? With one article you could reach exponentially more than you could by networking alone.

You can also get media attention. Read periodicals

that reach your target audience to see how and what they cover. See how your experience can be tailored to fit. You should ask them if they might be interested in you as an accessible expert, the embodiment of a problem-solving process. Or you might ask if they would be interested in you as an interesting personality (giving yourself an intriguing hook).

You want to present them with something significant, interesting, and timely in your niche area so you can address your specific audience. To do this you would write to the specific editor that you have a good article angle or are a good story yourself as a problem solver along with good tips, inside information, or list of practical resources.

These approaches are advantageous. They give you the opportunity to see others making an effort to contact you because of your resources. They reinforce your self-confidence and perceptions of your worth as a contact. They create equity: While you are pursuing others, others are actively pursuing you.

In the words of Thomas Watson, Jr., former-president of IBM, "If you want to be a big company tomorrow, you have to start acting like one today."

19

IT'S RELATIONSHIP-BASED MARKETING

To create opportunities and achieve your goals you need to be able to step outside your own skin and comfort zone. One way to do this is to look objectively at yourself and what benefits you offer to others. What you offer in the marketplace of work or personal relationships is a "commodity." It can be your talent, abilities, experience, expertise, a service, or product, but it's still a "commodity."

This means, you literally must think of yourself as an entity to be offered to the public (including organizations). This is because they will be thinking of you that way. Furthermore, doing so makes it easier for you to objectively assess yourself.

Effective self-promotion requires that you market, or "sell," yourself. I know for many people the ideal of "selling," especially "selling yourself," is repugnant. It smacks of slick manipulation and hustling to get what you want at the expense of the other person. But this isn't that kind of "selling." This "selling" involves people interacting for the purpose of exploring and filling mutual needs and wants, like an extension of networking.

Instead, think of this "selling" as a form of *relationship-based marketing* which is a strategy for connecting strongly with people through open communication suited to their interests, needs, and wants for a long-term engagement and customer loyalty. Some refer to this as "soft-sell marketing." An excellent reference to this approach is *The Heart of Marketing: Love Your Customers and They Will Love You Back* by Drs. Judith Sherven and Jim Sniechowski. Your purpose is to get others to know, like, and trust you, to present your benefits to them, and then *let them decide* if what you're "selling" is what they are "buying."

According to Martin Luther King Jr., "Life's most persistent and urgent question is, 'What are you doing for others?'"

As a relationship-based self-promoter, you start by listening carefully to the buyer. You discern their problem then create a solution to it. This requires your attention to problem solving, creativity, and sensitivity to others' needs, wants, and moods.

Contact making is, in fact, really an unstructured "sales interaction," in which neither the prospective seller nor the prospective buyer knows exactly how to help the other at the start of the situation. It is then through mutual examination that you uncover the wants and opportunities. Therefore, to promote, market or sell your resources and benefits, you must

- Know specifically and concretely what you have to offer that others want

- Develop the rapport first and be open to giving first
- Know your self-promotion style and how to adapt it to the situation
- Seek out and qualify new prospects by what you can exchange
- Know each potential consumer and their business
- Know as much as you can about the consumer's problem
- Know the consumer's buying style
- Know how to work with their style for best results
- Have a plan to reach your goal in mind
- Give yourself a timeline for achieving each objective
- Develop proposals to present to initiate an exchange
- Market yourself subtly in person, emphasizing benefits you're providing
- Ask for what you want in the context of what you're willing to give
- Follow up on all marketing efforts, whether career or persona
- Keep contacts warm even when not actively exchanging.

Since people buy the perceived benefits of a product or entity (e.g., the status of having a BMW) and not the features of the product itself (the vehicle itself), you need to look at yourself and ask, "What benefits do people see me offering to them? What emotional wants can my resources ultimately fill?"

You aim at their "wants" because people recognize

and act on those but don't necessarily know or act on their "needs." Though you are offering your expertise, information, skills, abilities, support, guidance or connections, what you really are marketing is the value that having access to your resources can provide. It's how they will feel about some achievement and what it can provide them psychologically. You are selling the opportunity for others to get what they want through you—an equitable *quid pro quo*.

Note: Always remember that people buy from emotion then rationalize the purchase with logic.

EFFECTIVE PERSONAL MARKETING

When you know what benefits you represent to others and specifically which ones you want to promote in order to achieve your goals, you are ready to begin the marketing process. Effective relationship marketing is often thought of as transfer of enthusiasm. You package and present your wares with an enthusiasm that creates enthusiastic acceptance of them by others.

Effective relationship marketing requires that you not think of the interaction as a short-term buy-and-sell situation. It's important that you keep in mind that your objective is, instead, always a long-term, ongoing relationship of a service and trust exchange.

Effective relationship marketing requires you being seen as legitimate. You need to preface everything with establishment of your credibility. You do this by demonstrating your relevant reputation, experience, expertise, and the confidence in yourself to use them effectively. You need to demonstrate a strong knowledge and understanding of the buyer's situation, needs and wants. But most of all you need to project value—that there is no fluff, only solid benefits for your buyer. Your projecting these qualities makes others feel more comfortable with you and more receptive to you. It inspires trust in you so you can create that trust relationship.

Effective relationship marketing (self-promotion) also requires that you make no initial assumptions about what your buyer does or does not know. Always make your presentation simple, direct, and complete. This will make you immediately understandable, irrespective of the situation. This approach applies whether your buyer is an organizational decision maker or potential contact.

Remember: It is important that you make it easy for people to buy what you have to offer, whatever it is you have to offer.

IMPRESSION MANAGEMENT

Effective relationship marketing is all about image. It requires that you create impressions of yourself that draw a favorable response. Impression management refers to how you create and manage the impressions you give off in interacting with others, the role you assume, and the behaviors you use in accord with the situation at hand. It consists of

- What you do
- How you do it
- What you say
- How you say it.

Part of this created image also is how you respond to

these roles and behaviors in other people. Is the buyer acting like a friend who is showing concern about your life problems? Is the buyer acting like a parent who is telling you what you should do to succeed?

A third part of creating impressions is building on any shared characteristics, interests, affiliations, or acquaintances. For example, if you both are conservatives, Democrats, joggers, like broccoli au gratin, attended Texas A & M, read John Grisham, root for the Red Sox, ride a Harley, are cat lovers, or know Oprah personally, you have the basis for making a good impression. Why? Because you are sharing something that captures the buyer's attention: common interests. Common interests create a bond.

Perceived similarities increase the positive identification between you and the buyer. They build desire for further interaction which, in turn, should lead to a sale— in this case, making a contact, locating a piece of information or a mentor, or getting a job interview.

An easy way to remember the components of the "selling" process is the marketing acronym **AIDA**: You present the product (you) in a way that

- Gains the buyer's **Attention**
- Holds the buyer's **Interest**
- Builds the buyer's **Desire**
- Prompts the buyer's **Action**, a purchase: job or contact.

YOUR SELF-PROMOTION AND "SALES" FORMULA

To lead the buyer to an acceptance of you as a contact (a purchase), there are specific things that you need to do. The most effective "sales" formula revolves around your product's

- Identification
- Benefits
- Values
- Comfort
- Features
- Advantages over the competition
- Trust
- Likability
- Empathy
- Relevant anecdotes/stories
- Demonstration of willingness and ability to solve the problem.

When you offer your resource to others, you want to point to the buyer's problem or want and how what you offer is an effective, efficient solution (by showing the bottom line results you've achieved on a similar problem). While features of your product are undoubtedly important to the buyer (such as, your specific computer experience at Apple), what you want to show to the potential buyer is the advantage of this feature (indicating how your direct connection with people at Apple is helpful). You want to point out how the feature and its inherent advantages benefit the buyer (knowing the right people at Apple can get you in to see decision makers ASAP).

You want to create an empathetic sales narrative

that makes those benefits visible in the buyer's terms ("Knowing that you're presenting your ideas to people who are ready and able to make a decision on them creates confidence."). Finally, you want to demonstrate proof of what your benefit narrative claims ("Claudia M., who had a new graphics software idea, was referred to Stan Q., special assistant to the president, who was looking for innovative graphics designers. As a result, she got a plum assignment").

WALTER L.'S PERSONAL MARKETING TECHNIQUE

Walter L. is a problem solver just entering the field of consulting. He knows that writing articles can help him establish his credibility as an authority. It can also promote his service. As a result, he decides to write a series of articles on the problem-solving process. The articles lead the reader step-by-step through the difficulties of the process and suggest expeditious methods to overcome them. They point out the benefits to the reader of effectively, efficiently, and economically solving problems.

While the purpose of the series is both educational and public service, the articles are in reality promotional literature for Walter. They whet the reader's appetite for his services by telling them just enough to help them get a good, solid start, but are not enough to totally substitute for his consulting. They constitute free advertising which suggests that if the readers want to go further to advance, it would be of further benefit to them to have Walter implement his advice for them.

MARKETING YOURSELF IS MOSTLY LISTENING

To "sell" yourself effectively you must be prepared to listen, and listen *actively*. You want to hear what the buyer wants to buy. They will tell you if you give them the chance. Thus, you want to make sure that you do not monopolize the conversation.

It is easy to become enamored of the sound of your own voice. But remember that your potential buyers feel the same way about their own voices. To create a good impression and gather the information you want and need it is better to encourage them to talk, talk, and talk. Asking them questions is a particularly powerful way to do this.

Note: Asking intelligent, insightful questions of the right people has provided some individuals with jobs, promotions, financial backing, and the sale of their products and services. They know what they want so let them tell you!

When others talk, be sure not to interrupt. You must let the speaker finish their thought. It is likely to be a good opening for your next and deeper question. Similarly, you should be concentrating on what they are saying, and not thinking about what you are going to say next.

When you jump in to continue talking, your behavior will not be seen as enthusiasm. Rather, it will suggest that you have not been listening. It will be seen as bad manners (although this may vary with regional culture). Inattentiveness and discourtesy are two big no-no's for creating and promoting a good image.

To market yourself effectively you need to master

concepts, skills, attitudes, and habits that improve your proficiency in influencing prospects to make a positive buying decision. According to the nationally-known motivational consultant and lecturer Zig Ziglar, "Every presentation involves a sale. Either the seller sells the prospect on buying, or the prospect sells the seller on not buying." When you think about the relationship you're creating, think about it in terms of creating a *friend*, not a "buyer."

20

MAINTENANCE TACTICS

Your new mantra should be what scientist Louis Pasteur knew only too well: "Chance favors the prepared mind."

There are eleven important points to keep in mind as you move from job holder—career survivalist to job holder—to career success. Even when you have learned all the strategies and perfected the techniques so that you can pull opportunities seemingly out of the air when you want them, you may fall back on early ingrained habits of jumping to conclusions, impatience, procrastination, and lack of assertiveness. It's easy to do when you're first getting started. Consequently, referring to these maintenance tactics every now and then will make such temporary regression less likely and, if it occurs, significantly less severe—eventually disappearing.

ESTABLISH YOUR PRIORITIES

If you are to achieve your goals, you must continually rank-order those things you need to do to accomplish them. This means sometimes asking hard questions of yourself and making tough decisions. For example, deciding whether just to have fun at an important trade show or association event or actively working at contact-making. You have to determine what is important to achieving your goals at any given moment and then act on it.

TAKE THE INITIATIVE

You absolutely must be assertive. Being able to go after what you want and to stand up for your rights in doing so often requires "reprogramming" yourself. You must be able to express your desires to others. You must be able to say "Yes" when you really want to say it. You must know how to and be able to say "No" when you really want to say that too. However, assertiveness decisions need to have both a gut and logical component. Sometimes you may not feel like doing something that your logic tells you that you really need to do.

Remember: Assertiveness is not aggressiveness.

Aggressiveness is demanding your rights in an unreasonable manner and at the expense of others. It is feeling angry and frustrated with yourself and others. In order to feel good about asking for what you want, you need to feel good about yourself. And you need to believe that you have the right to achieve your goals (so long as achieving them does not infringe on the rights of others). Furthermore, *only* you can make certain that your aspirations and accomplishments are made known to potential contacts and decision makers. You are responsible for your visibility, credibility, and actions.

SPEAK UP

Polish your ability to speak before others. This goes beyond the art of small talk, although you need to achieve that too. (For more information on mastering small talk and fear of speaking check out *How to Speak Without Fear Small Talk Course* on Kindle.) When you speak, you want to

- Hold the other's attention
- Capture their interest
- Create similarities and familiarity toward developing a rapport
- Use stories or anecdotes to demonstrate empathy, benefits, and value
- Build their desire
- Lead them to some action.

Practice expressing yourself by

- Introducing yourself in an intriguing way
- Describing what you have and want
- Asking insightful, intelligent questions
- Drawing out the other person to discern their wants.

The better you project yourself when speaking, the more visible you will be, the better you will market yourself, and the better you will be remembered the next time.

ACCEPT RESPONSIBILITY FOR YOUR ACTIONS

If you are to get what you want, you must master your destiny. The choices are yours. The decisions are yours. President Harry S Truman's succinct pronouncement applies: "The buck stops here." (By the way, in case you were wondering, there is no period after the "*S*" in Harry S̲ Truman. Truman had no middle name. The "S" stood for two relatives whose names began with "S.") If you make a mistake, you make a mistake. It is a fact of life. You are a fallible human being. (Sorry, there are no other options available.) And fallible human beings make mistakes, lots of them!

Do not make excuses for your mistakes. Do not shift the blame to something outside yourself ("It wasn't my fault. The Devil made me do it!"). Accept responsibility for the error, learn something from it, let go of the emotion, live with it, and move on.

Remember: Executives who make only 50% of their decisions correctly can still be successful.

You learn by doing. Treat mistakes as occasions for learning. And though you do learn through insight, you learn mostly through trial and error. Thus, you should etch on the inside of your skull the following motto: "I am not perfect and never will be (and neither is anyone else … ha, ha!)"

Believe it or not, in general, other people really do not expect you to be perfect. Why? It is because other people tend to be more objective about you. That is, they tend to be more realistic than that about your human limitations.

Unfortunately, those same individuals who give latitude to others tend not to be so objective about their own limitations. (Sound familiar?) While they are allowing you realistic slack as a human being, they too are expecting themselves to be perfect, much to their own disappointment and frustration.

It is a strange paradox. While your expectations of others tend to be realistic, objective, and flexible, with reasonable standards, your expectations of yourself tend to be unrealistic, subjective, and rigid, with unreasonably high standards.

According to philosopher and architect R. Buckminster Fuller, "Mistakes are sins, only when *not* admitted." This means you *must* allow yourself to be human and make errors. Mistakes are the way you learn what works and what does not. These are data which are essential to your progress as a human and worker. They help you grow and develop.

Would you like me to give you a formula for success? According to IBM's Thomas Watson, Sr., "If you want to increase your success rate, double your failure rate." Simple but seemingly contradictory. It sounds incongruous because we all tend to think of failure as the enemy of success. But it absolutely is not. Think about it. You can be discouraged by failure *or* you can learn from it.

What this says is go ahead and make mistakes. Make all you can. Make them as fast as you can. Seriously! The sooner you see what does not work the sooner you will discover what does.

Also, according to Watson, Sr., "You find your success on the other side of your mistakes."

As Thomas Edson said about failure, "I have not failed. I've just found 10,000 ways that won't work. ... Many of life's failures are people who did not realize how close they were to success when they gave up."

And when you make mistakes, you need to keep your

self-confidence high and remember that you are doing what is necessary to do to get your correct answer. In the process you will encounter obstacles, things you will want to change. However, be aware that you cannot change everything, that everything is not under your control to change it. As a result, you have to resolve to change *only* what you can and not dwell on what you cannot change.

Furthermore, *if only* applies only if you have the power to go back in time to alter events. Sad to say, you do not have that option. This means you need to accept your full responsibility and learn all you can from it. This is the classic example of making lemonade from lemons.

MAKE NO NEGATIVE ASSUMPTIONS

Never assume who can or cannot provide what and when. You literally never know from where a lead, piece of important information, or support can come. Work to overcome the human tendency to see others one-dimensionally even if you know them well. Be aware, think outside the box, and open to possibilities. Hold your labeling and evaluation in abeyance. Judgments can get in the way and prevent your exploring fertile territory where opportunities may lurk around every corner or under every bush. Do not prejudge but explore. Surprising discoveries await you.

BE PATIENT

Contact making takes time, especially when you begin. Before you actively ask for what you want, you need to build the foundation of giving and creating relationships so others get to know you and your expertise, experience, skills, and abilities. Then as they get to know, like, trust you, and see you as sincere and authentic, your network grows and connections are made more rapidly. Leads materialize when you least expect them. As long as you stay aware and open to them, you can take advantage of them.

Remember: Impatience creates frustration and anxiety and does not speed up the process.

On the contrary, impatience creates negativity which is communicated to your potential contacts. It bogs you down by distracting you, blurring your focus, and taking your eye off your goal. This not only creates a negative impression and impedes your growth but also can blind you to career- and life opportunity doors that are ajar.

KEEP EXPANDING YOUR NETWORK

Always look for other avenues to explore as well. Ask your contacts, "Can you suggest anyone else I might talk to about this?" Be sure to pass their names along to others who may benefit from them. This will further increase your visibility and credibility and enhance existing as well as new relationships.

KEEP CONTACTS ALIVE

Making the initial contact is not enough. You need to keep your contacts warm, whether they are new or well-established. Your goal is to create a personal relationship. If you have let them cool, rekindle them. You can send an e-mail or call merely to say, "Hello."

Send an e-mail or call to discuss an area of mutual interest. Send the person a note to say, "Hi, I have not seen you in a while and I was thinking about you." Send the person a clipping or notice related to their interest, a job opportunity, marketing lead, or something humorous.

Also send a birthday, anniversary, congratulations, condolence, or holiday card. People find this very personal and meaningful, further reinforcing their positive impression of you. Be sure to accompany what you send if it is less personal with a brief, personal note.

Personal notes always trump impersonal e-mails. You want to show you value them and care about them even when not actively in an exchange.

Remember: You have to have a personal relationship with them irrespective of what they provide you in any exchange.

SHOW YOUR GRATITUDE

You need to appreciate and be grateful for what you receive from your network. Your contacts are choosing to assist you; they don't have to. Consequently, you need to supply support and enthusiasm to your contacts. Be both a source and resource of information. Whenever possible, try to act as matchmaker and pair people with specific *wants* with others with specific complementary *haves*. This reinforces the gratitude of others for you as well.

MAKE THE MOST OF ANY OPPORTUNITIES

When opportunities arise, **do not wait** ... not for a moment. Career- and life doors open and close quickly. They change with changes in the environment. These are factors you are unlikely to be able to predict or have much control over them. Therefore, you must act immediately. Yes, there will always be another opportunity coming your way, but you can't be sure when and what each opportunity represents. That means when one appears, ACT! No pussy-footing around!

Success comes to those who are on the lookout for those openings. Success comes to those who are prepared to stride confidently through those doors when they find them. Success comes to those who then act on their expectations, their preparation, and each specific opportunity.

START NETWORKING NOW!

Even if you do not feel the need to have contacts right now, you must realize that "having an active network" is not an automatic happening. You cannot plug into an effective network overnight. You cannot build an active network in a hurry. Yes, you have your core network with family and friends etc., but it still takes time to get them up to speed and helping you.

Networking requires time and effort on your part to create visibility and credibility as well as relationships based on knowing, liking, and trusting. Moreover, just because you suddenly are ready for accessing contacts does not necessarily mean that your contacts will suddenly be ready for you. You will have little control over timing of the actions of others.

When you have a problem to resolve right away, it is already too late to start the networking process to solve it. In addition, both cultivating contacts and solving problems can be initially somewhat stressful. By having your network in place and available when you need it, you both lighten your problem-solving burden and reduce your associated stress.

VALUE YOURSELF

It is easier to promote and sell a product in which you believe than one in which you do not. It is easier to promote and "sell" a product which you value. Chances are that if you could see your resources in another individual, you would be favorably impressed. You could see expertness, depth, intensity, diversity, and value of both the organizational and personal qualities.

Be as good to yourself as you would be to that someone else with those resources you consider worthy. It is not egotistical to appreciate those attributes, skills, abilities, and experience that just happen to belong to you. They are valuable and desirable irrespective of to whom they belong.

You are not an imposter when you promote yourself as unique and valuable. Because you are just that! What you are is realistic and practical. **If you do not appreciate yourself and all the resources you have to offer others, no one else will either.** This is because you will project your degree of self-appreciation in your look, approach, words, and behavior. Others then will

reflect your perception of yourself, much like the reflection in a mirror. I
f your perception of yourself isn't one of worth, others will be less willing to network with you.

Remember: If you make a mistake, it's no big deal. Everyone makes mistakes ... lots of them. Besides, it's how you learn and succeed.

As I mentioned earlier, it's better to make as many mistakes as fast as you can because it puts you on a higher learning curve. You've discovered what works and what doesn't. So, when you make an error,

- Examine it
- Ask yourself what it tells you
- If you need to do something about it, do it
- Ask yourself what you might do differently next time
- Then chuck any negative emotion you may have about it because you can't go back in time to change it. Feeling bad serves no purpose and just interferes with your progress. You can "change" it in the future by not repeating it.

If you believe you have the benefits to satisfy the wants of others and if you make it known to the world that you want to share those benefits with them, the results will be overwhelming. The world will beat a path to your door to reap the harvest of those benefits. If you truly believe and project that belief, they will believe it too! As a result, they will want to share with you and help you get what you want.

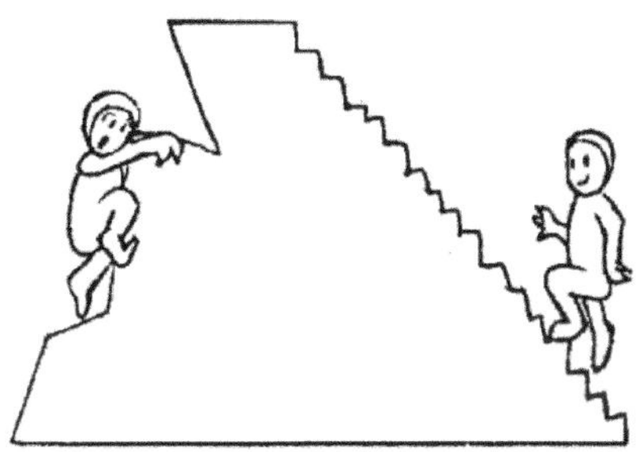

OTHER JOB-SEARCH-RELEVANT E-COURSES

To further assist you to more confidently achieve your job-getting goal I have additional job-hunt-related books that can give you that competitive edge.

My *What No One Has Told You: How Insiders Really Get Jobs* includes:

- <u>Determining your job goal</u> ("What Are You Really Looking for in a Job?")
- <u>Researching the job</u> ("Why Do I Have to Research the Job Market?")
- <u>Résumés</u> ("Create a Résumé but Don't Send It?")
- <u>Interviews</u> ("You've Gotten the Interview Appointment: Now What?!")
- <u>Job-screen testing</u> ("You Want to Test My 'What?'")
- <u>Job decision making</u> ("You've Gotten the Job Offer: Now What?")

OTHER RESOURCES

Signe A. Dayhoff, PhD, *How to Speak Without Fear Small Talk Course*

Signe A. Dayhoff, PhD, *Scared of Your Boss? Smash Through Your Fear Now!*

Wendy Gelberg, *The Successful Introvert*

Laurie Schloff, *Smart Speaking: 60-Second Strategies for More Than 100 Speaking Problems and Fears*

Judith Sherven and Jim Sniechowski, *The Heart of Marketing: Love Your Customers and They Will Love You Back*

Judith Sherven and Jim Sniechowski—*Overcoming the Fear of Being Fabulous*

21

THE CONCLUSION?
IT IS ONLY THE BEGINNING!

With this book you can not only survive but also succeed as a job holder and career builder:

- You can get what you want
- You can develop yourself
- You can advance
- You can do whatever you choose to do because this book provides you with the knowledge, tools, and guidance you need.

But *you* have to provide the desire, the motivation, and the effort. Your success requires thorough preparation, persistence, and lots of perspiration on your part. Your success requires that you **conscientiously follow** and **act on** the guidelines presented in this book.

It would be wonderful if everyone who reads this book would become "successful." However, I suspect that this will not be the case. Why? It is because some people:

- Are too afraid to try
- Do not believe they can accomplish what they

desire
- Are not willing to do the exercises
- Are not ready to take control of their lives
- Want immediate gratification
- Are not willing to exercise the patience to build the necessary foundation for their success.

Thus, while I guarantee these methods, which have been systematically tested and proved over the last 35-plus years, I do not—and cannot—guarantee your individual belief in yourself and in the process; your willingness to act; or your effort to implement every step of the process. *Only **you** can do that.*

But, if you take the information and suggestions to heart, do each and every exercise, apply them to your own self-promotion and goal-achievement program, and then **practice, practice, practice**, success in creating opportunities and opening career- and life doors will be all yours.

WHAT CONSTITUTES YOUR SUCCESS?

Your *success* is
- Knowing your resources
- Valuing your resources
- Knowing your goals
- Knowing what resources you need to access to achieve your goals
- Having a concrete, specific, measurable, achievable plan
- Alleviating anxiety and stress to bolster mastery and confidence
- Taking risks and making decisions

- Visualizing your success constantly
- Being approachable
- Telling everyone what you want to achieve
- Developing visibility and credibility
- Tooting your own horn so others can see and appreciate you
- Creating a positive self-image
- Developing self-confidence
- Thinking in terms of creating *relationships*, not "selling"
- Making true personal relationships the basis of all you do
- Being committed to sharing with others ... first
- Keeping your motivation going
- Accepting mistakes and "failures" as getting you closer to your goal
- Determining what kinds of contacts you need to access
- Networking for those contacts
- Knowing that networking is sharing and not exploiting
- Being grateful for what you receive
- Showing gratitude and sincere appreciation
- Remaining alert and open to opportunities
- Not prejudging what contacts can provide
- Showing a positive attitude and enthusiasm
- Being assertive in following your path to get what you want
- Making effective small talk a priority
- Creating an "elevator speech" to introduce

yourself interestingly
- Looking for commonalties and similarities on which to bond
- Listening actively to make interactions most useful
- Developing rapport and relationship with contacts
- Working toward contacts knowing, liking, and trusting you
- Doing research on people and companies wherever possible
- Preparing yourself for each interaction
- Initiating conversations
- Having a short list of things to talk about
- Acting like a host, not a guest
- Communicating effectively
- Communicating frequently to let people know you're thinking of them
- Exit conversations and relationships graciously—never burn bridges
- Speaking publicly to gain further visibility and credibility
- Using the media to further your reputation and worth
- Managing your time and actions to be both efficient and effective
- Knowing that your success is the result of your beliefs, attitudes, thoughts, feelings, and actions
- Knowing that you are responsible for creating what you want
- Practicing each and every suggestion, tip, recommendation

- Noting every single success, no matter how small
- Rewarding yourself for every success
- Monitoring your accomplishing your plan.

Your success is constantly learning, updating, and practicing this material and all its recommendations. *Don't read it once. Don't do the exercises once.*

The more you incorporate this method into your thinking and acting, the more skilled and confident you'll become.

The more you incorporate this method into your thinking and acting, the more quickly and effectively you'll accomplish each and every goal you formulate.

As a **Success**, you will

- Feel the thrill of creating your own opportunities—not only career or job but also personal
- Feel the satisfaction of a more competent, assertive, and effective you
- Feel the confidence of your taking control and accomplishing your goals
- Become thrilled, satisfied, and invigorated by a new-found sense of self-mastery in all areas of your personal and work life
- Know that you are no longer relegated to being just a face in the crowd, spinning your wheels like so many others
- Know that you are someone who can and does create your own destiny.

Now when the question of "Promote myself?" comes to mind, you won't respond, "I'd rather eat worms!" Instead, you'll shout, *"You bet your sweet _______!"*

BRAVO! CONGRATULATIONS! YOU DESERVE IT!

Here's wishing you self-promotion success for *anything* you want to achieve!

ABOUT THE AUTHOR

Signe A. Dayhoff, Ph.D., is a social psychologist, Social-Effectiveness Coach, and cognitive behaviorist who received her doctorate from Boston University. She began doing publicity for the American Cancer Society and personal marketing consulting for solo business people and service providers.

While teaching Social Psychology and Organizational Behavior & Development at University of Massachusetts, Boston University, and Framingham State College (now University of Framingham), she produced and hosted, Continental Cablevision's alternative-career-development–personal marketing program, the *Inside Track*, in Wellesley, Massachusetts, for four years. For it she received a Conti Award nomination.

She is the author of 13 related books, including:

- *Create Your Own Career Opportunities*, a guide to self-promotion through creating visibility and credibility, used at Pepperdine University
- *Diagonally-Parked in a Parallel Universe: Working Through Social Anxiety* (2nd Edition), acclaimed by leading clinical researchers and therapists in the field
- *Get the Job You Want: Successful Strategies for Selling Yourself in the Job Market*

- *How to Win in a Tough Job Market: Successful Strategies for Getting the Job You Want*
- *What No One Told You: How Insiders Really Get Jobs*
- *Scared of Your Boss? Smash Through Your Fear Now Course*
- *How to Speak Without Fear Small Talk Course*
- *Single and Multiple Mentors: Perceived Effects on Managerial Success*
- *Decision Making for Managers* (for AMACOM's Education for Management).
- Contributed to books such as Steven J. Bennett's *Executive Chess: Creative Problem Solving by 45 of America's Top Business Leaders and Thinkers.*

She founded The Mentoring Network to show individuals how to communicate, present, and personally promote themselves more confidently and effectively to engineer their success. Having done extensive research on such issues as mentoring, networking, effective interpersonal communication, social intelligence, and social anxiety reduction, she has presented her findings nationally, in person and on radio and television. She also chaired the Task Force on Mentoring for the American Psychological Association and created a mentoring program for the headquarters of the American Red Cross.

She has been quoted in publications including *Industry Week, Wall Street Journal, Success, Executive Travel, Time Out New York, Shape,* and *Cosmopolitan,* and has written for the *Boston Business Journal.*

She is also an applied feline behaviorist, "kitty mom" to 20-plus rescued elderly, disabled, and chronically-ill cats, and is author of four cat memoirs:

- *What Faust the Dancing Cat Taught Me*
- *Faust the Dancing Cat Tackles Strippers, Scammers & Bears*
- *Faust the Dancing Cat Does Vegas*
- *Remarkable Tales of Cats Who Whisper to Humans*
- *How Intrepid the Disabled Kitten Triumphed to Help Others.*